Pedagogy of the Heart

Pedagogy of the Heart

The Psychological and Political Memoirs of a Master Teacher

Martin L. Kokol

HAMILTON BOOKS
AN IMPRINT OF
ROWMAN & LITTLEFIELD
Lanham • Boulder • New York • London

Published by Hamilton Books
An imprint of The Rowman & Littlefield Publishing Group, Inc.
4501 Forbes Boulevard, Suite 200, Lanham, Maryland 20706
www.rowman.com

86-90 Paul Street, London EC2A 4NE, United Kingdom

British Library Cataloguing in Publication Information Available

Library of Congress Cataloging-in-Publication Data

Names: Kokol, Martin, author.
Title: Pedagogy of the heart : the psychological and political memoirs of a master
    teacher / Martin Kokol.
Description: Lanham, Maryland : Hamilton Boos, an imprint of Rowman & Littlefield,
    2022. | Includes bibliographical references and index. | Summary: "This work is
    offered at a most critical time in American K–12 education, where we are facing a
    generation connected to technology like no other before them, begging educators to
    consider reconceptualizing the focus of their work. The author invites the reader to
    ponder a very different look at his work"— Provided by publisher.
Identifiers: LCCN 2022002845 (print) | LCCN 2022002846 (ebook) | ISBN
    9780761873167 (paperback) | ISBN 9780761873174 (epub)
Subjects: LCSH: Education—United States. | Teaching—United States.
Classification: LCC LA217.2 .K655 2022 (print) | LCC LA217.2 (ebook) | DDC
    370.973—dc23/eng/20220222
LC record available at https://lccn.loc.gov/2022002845
LC ebook record available at https://lccn.loc.gov/2022002846

To Ari, Natalie and Katie
Grateful to you all the days of my life!

Contents

Acknowledgments

I wish to begin by thanking my parents, Harold and Vivian, now both gone, for honoring my initial desire to take on the work of teaching adolescents, and then supporting me financially, with helpful support required during a doctoral run and even in helping me with a couple of physical relocations. Their support was nothing short of monumental, considering the culture's expectations to work New York corporate that were in place from the beginning of my own early adulthood, as they trusted me to write my own script. In the same breadth, taking place at a similar time, I also want to thank Mrs. Judy Chasanoff, dear friend to my mother, who, after walking with me for a few hours one late December day, helped me to gain the courage to speak my truth and to declare the intentions of my heart—to teach.

Before I mention professional relationships that secured my place here, there have been extraordinary friendships that have also guided my career, relationships that have been just as important in the long run. Alas, this recognition might be unusual, but it is my story. Dr. Jill Baron has been one over the last three decades, indeed a friend from childhood. Dr. Scott Jones has been not just a college roommate, but also someone I could confide in with my journey and its challenges. There are also a few former students with whom I have had the privilege of building life-long friendships, after being their high school teacher at Palmer School in Miami 35–40 years ago. Dr. Christopher Hoyt, faculty at Western Carolina University, has been such a friend. Joshua Tarjan, Phil Lopez, Eddie Montilla, Chad Peters—these men grew as I grew and encouraged me not to give up the calling.

Then, later on, there were a few whom I taught as a rookie university professor almost 25 years ago at Brigham Young University. Eric Campbell and Shahram Paksima, both wonderfully entrenched in their careers, provided a safe place in which to share our professional journeys. Further along, colleagues in New York City offered me steady and significant support as I took on being an urban teacher educator. Laurie Bobley, Lorli Dima Ala and Ron Lehrer, two colleagues as well as my direct boss at Touro College were powerful influencers for me to step up and give it my all, quietly reminding me that I had lots to learn and not just teach. Ron's support in granting me additional work allowed me to stay in New York.

Colleagues at Teton High School have been wonderful, as, once again, I am quite the outsider to the cultures that are present here in eastern Idaho. Lisie Smith has been a fellow northeasterner who has helped me to step up at many turns in my time here. Brent Schindler has been the wonderful colleague that everyone needs at work in order to succeed. Both of them encouraged me to write my own script, as I returned to the world of secondary education, both to enjoy the break from higher education and to find times to document my time as a novice high school teacher once again—which would lead to more serious writing.

But, it has been Dr. Clifford Mayes, academic psychologist and curriculum theorist, wonderful colleague during my BYU years, extraordinary friend since the onset of social media, and now my cherished intellectual support in order to get this work out to being published. I am grateful beyond words for his solid belief in my skills, in my life's journey, and in the need for me to secure my voice in the world of education, and not just with a new area code besides me!

But, in the end, the ones that blessed me beyond any measure that I could quantify are my three phenomenal daughters, Arianna, Natalie and Katherine, now with their guys. What each of them gave me across their lifespan has been a complete acceptance of their father's calling. No matter how many times I was a bit late for dinner. No matter how many people they would meet, as I might have had a class over for a special occasion. No matter how far away I would need to live in order to continue the work of being an educator.

And while it was such a joy to be able to hop on a nonstop JFK to SLC flight to be there for graduations and for birthdays, they always shared with me the excitement of my work, and the stories I might have for them. They have no doubt helped to keep me young in spirit. And we have enjoyed our times at every turn. The patience they offered me was far beyond their years, stretching them mightily. I am eternally grateful for each of them, being daughters whom I love so much—that I can now begin to understand how Tevye, from Fiddler on the Roof, could feel about his three!

Introduction

What Is a Teacher?

Over the past forty years as a high school teacher and then as a doctoral student, and then as a university professor and then again as a high school teacher, I gradually, silently, almost unwittingly, became fascinated by what educational theorists call the "null curriculum" (Eisner and Vallance 1986). What is that funny-sounding beast? Why would I begin a book with "Null"?

Well, in the parlance of the curriculum theorist (and that is one of the hats I wear, as you will see me don and doff various hats in our journey together), the null curriculum is the material that is not in the curriculum although some might argue that it should have been. But then again, isn't it often the case in many conversations that what is not said is every bit as important as what is said, and sometimes even more important? It's that grinning half-ton gorilla sitting in the corner that no one mentions. Let's make matters clear from the outset and talk about the gorilla!

Or, in a subtle variation on the null curriculum, an item, topic, person, practice, or what have you, *may* appear on the physical or virtual page of the curriculum, but it matters very little if the teacher cunningly evades it. Generally, a student will never see the null curriculum, will not even know it could have been there—and that is just the intent of those who left it out . . . if, that is, they left it out purposefully. At any rate, the null curriculum is the stuff that does not make it to the pages of the curriculum given the student (and more accurately, often enough imposed upon him or her) at the beginning of the term.

Often, the teacher ignores it, deflects any discussion of it, and even makes it known in explicit or implicit ways that she will not be happy and that there may be consequences to the student or students who choose to press the matter. Curriculum theory explains this phenomenon by saying that although such-and-such a thing is part of what is called "the official curriculum," the teacher is negating it by what *she* decides will and won't be taught. This we call "the operational curriculum."

Some studies (Cuban 1993) suggest that the teacher's operational curriculum grows with experience; that is, the longer she teaches, the greater her confidence that *he or she* knows better than the State with its "official curriculum" what "her" students really need to know. Thus, a first-year teacher will draw 95% of her curriculum from the State's official curriculum (Bullough, 2009), whereas for a veteran teacher of 25 years, only 10%–20% of the curriculum he delivers in his operational curriculum will come from the State. The rest is what he has put together for his students over the years (Cuban 1993)

The null and operational curriculum are not always bad—the products of evil intent or ignorance. A teacher who ignores a section of a book that argues that concentration camps in World War Two were a myth and are part of an ongoing "Jewish conspiracy" to exaggerate their suffering for crafty political gain would be exercising real pedagogical wisdom and moral courage in making those things part of the null curriculum in her class, and doing so by the exercise of her right as a teacher to operationalize (the operational curriculum just mentioned) the official curriculum she was given in a way she deemed best for her students.

There are even more dimensions to the curriculum. Take, for instance, the "hidden curriculum." This is the message that the teacher communicates to the students about how she feels about herself, her students, and the topics under analysis in the classroom, for those three things often combine in subtle ways that are impossible to define but, everywhere present and at work in the classroom, and are impossible to ignore. This implicit curriculum is of a piece with the style, the baggage that any teacher carries as part of himself or herself into the classroom. It can be good. It can be bad. It all depends. But it is rarely neutral.

Things are generally hidden for a reason. The hidden curriculum is crackling with electricity of emotions everywhere you look in the classroom—just as what is not said over the dinner table may be exactly what is on everybody's mind and what is ruining the delicious fare rather irrelevantly now spread before them and that they pick at with moody forks. How teachers and students see themselves, each other, and what is to be studied are not ancillary to the life of the classroom. They *are* the life of the classroom.

In my now long career in education as a theorist and practitioner, there have been several striking examples of this explicit or implicit curriculum that I have mused on over the years: the American history textbook that completely missed the point on what fueled Martin Luther King's mission; the controversial teacher who, unaware of emotional impact and ethical implications of his words, verbally assaulted (or at least demeaned) students with his firebrand of racist and sexist comments. These were easy to identify. But there are many that are much more subtle and only show up on the radar of one who has concerned himself with the various dimensions of the curriculum for a long time. I humbly suggest that I am such a person, and sharing with you some of my insights along these lines is a large slice of my motivation in writing this book.

Returning specifically to the issue of the null curriculum, I can tell you that what began in me as an uneasy sense of omission, a gap in the curriculum, has blossomed into a positive passion for identifying, bringing to everyone's awareness, and trying to deal with that part of an education that schools and even the larger society wish to ignore, whether out of ignorance or paranoia. This is the kind of thing a student in a college of education might hear about in a class in curriculum theory, but it only really hits home when you've been in the "trenches" a goodly time and see both the possibilities and the dangers (and frankly: mostly the dangers) of the null curriculum.

It is the great privilege (although a financial challenge) for all students preparing to become teachers that they go "out in the trenches"—that is, to be student teachers in the classroom itself. One learns a great deal in the trenches, and those lessons often come in the form of pithy expressions. The one I heard that did not merely catch my attention but educated me deeply came from Aristotle. He insisted that education can only be great if it combines heart and head, affect and cognition. Such an education, I reasoned, would need to be logically sound but also spiritually attuned to what the curricularist Phillip Phenix (1964) called the various "realms of meaning" that should comprise a truly well-rounded education.

This points to the many kinds of knowledge and the many contexts in which that knowledge operates that rounds intelligence out into its many interactive ethical forms, not merely unrelated cognitive shapes—that is, bits of information and decontextualized theories to learn for a good score on a standardized instrument . . . and forget as soon as the test is over. In other words, it is knowledge that is holistic and relevant to the child to live a vibrant, integral life, not merely preparing for the next standardized test. The teacher accomplishes this by following the general advice of veteran teachers to younger ones to "Keep your curriculum bright!"—which is to say: multifaceted and suffused with different kinds of light on each of its facets.

I had had the good fortune of teaching a whole bunch of very bright students in suburban Miami, some of whom had gone on to very selective colleges and universities in this country. But that gnawing feeling would not go away: If they were so smart, why were they so much in trouble with their personal lives? Why was their moral fabric torn in so many places? It had come time to address this matter. What I did not realize was that this deep concern would catapult me onto more rarefied intellectual playing fields in graduate schools of education, in which I would not be very comfortable with the rules of the academic games that are played there. I am a great fan of curriculum theory. But I am severely critical when it goes zooming off too high in the philosophical or political atmosphere and forget that, ultimately, all educational theory must revolve around very practical yet incomparably important questions of what is best for the child.

LAYING THE FIRST BRICKS OF A
MODEL OF EDUCATION

During these years of study, I often searched for ways in which to express to laypeople my concerns or to communicate my ideas for solutions to educational problems. I finally was able to accomplish this through illustration, through parable, or through some other modality. I often found that conventional scholarly prose for such highfalutin notions usually resulted in my turning a listener's initial interest into vague disinterest. So in order to elucidate my points and capture an audience's attention, I began to make use of visual models, simple but not simplistic, that I could quickly sketch out on a notebook pad. These visual aids became extremely useful in organizing this genre of idea to friends and family alike. Their use also forced me to make some sense, to clarify my thinking. To begin discussing the moral dimensions of a point, for I wanted to place it within the context of other, more familiar concepts.

And so, on the napkin, I placed the intellect on the left, the sentiment went on the right; and, if the spiritual was up top, then the physical was at bottom. Four squares arranged carefully, with the connection of the spiritual and the physical being defined as the soul. It might raise a few eyebrows, but then again, it was a start.

I knew, of course, that there had been many philosophers who had wrestled with various theories of knowledge in order to create their own theory of knowledge—or "epistemology," as this branch of philosophy is called. They also had to examine whether "reliable knowledge" came by reason or by revelation, whether by intuition or by sensing, whether by intellect or by sentiment or what we today incorrectly call "emotion."

The fun was in realizing that while everyone was quick to realize the importance of being moral, no one could suggest where this quality could best be explored in a curriculum. If "smarts" was a matter for the intellect, was morality a matter for the emotions? Certainly, it could not reside within the body (as anything carnal seemed to many people to smack of possible immorality). So, then, was it to be found in the spiritual? But, then, weren't we getting much too close to that great trap of straying into the world of religion?

Hence, a first word about where my search was allowed to venture: *anywhere truth was to be found!*

There were to be no "out of bounds" for this championship round. If I needed to reread the works of the great secular minds, so be it. But just as crucially, if I needed to inspect or even borrow from writers with a religious bent, then that would be allowable as well. A quick look at this book's bibliography will (I like to hope) reveal such eclecticism, such impartiality.

George Washington, in his Farewell Address of 1796, called religion and morality "the indispensable supports of political prosperity." He doubted that morality could be maintained without religion and suggested that these two are "the great pillars of public happiness and the firmest props of the duties of men and citizens" (Bellah 1976, 222).

Off I went, therefore, into the wilds of the search for a complete education. It is a journey of love in the service of education that I embarked on. In fact, I have never *not* been on this journey, nor will it ever end.

Let me just say, however, right up front, that the following criteria have always been, and, I imagine, always will be the general principles which give me joy and keep me moving forward against all odds and adversities. They are my *credo*:

First, teach from the head and also the heart. Learn by study and also by faith. *Gain an education, not just a training.*

Second, learn because there is more than yesterday; teach because there is a tomorrow, and engage as if there is only today. *Become a community of learners, not just a set of individuals preparing to take a test.*

Third, learn by doing and teach by being. *Ethical and existential progression, not just an accumulation of facts and unrelated theories, is what matters most in education.*

In this book, I invite the reader to hear tales—some exhilarating, some cautionary; some saddening, some uplifting—that will, I hope, educate him or her more deeply into their sense of calling as a teacher by expanding their vision of what education entails, by understanding the complete Existential reality it is for those of us who feel called to live "the pedagogical narrative" (Mayes 2020) under the pull of the "teaching mysteries" (Mayes 2004).

To that end, I seek to offer a much more complete picture of teaching than "specialized" books in "instructional theory" usually offer. Indeed, I hope to paint a picture for you, a lush landscape, wherein the grass and the shrubbery, the rocks and the flower beds all come together to complete the picture for a truly whole and deeply satisfying education—a landscape on which we can choose different spots to sit, each with different smells and lines of sight to enjoy as each spot delights and builds us up in different ways.

Now, I'd wager some, and maybe many, readers may be wondering if all this idealist talk about education is really for her or him. I humbly suggest it is—and this hope (yes, above all, *hope!*) in our admittedly fragile and fraught times, the still-exciting possibilities of education in America, is what I desire to show and share with you in what follows on our general sightseeing tour of the teeming world of revitalizing educational theory and practice in America.

Chapter 1

The Commitment and Calling of a Teacher

Yes, I am aware of the significant association of the initials of my name with a great figure in history. My full name is Martin Lawrence Kokol. My initials: MLK. They have inspired me since I was an elementary school student, home from school, taking a breather from practicing the piano, before my father got home from the mill. You see, I was quite aware of the man who was on the TV in the kitchen that late afternoon. His dream became my dream. Even more, his dream became my reality.

And if there was something deep within me that lasted throughout the decades, it was that reality. It was the part of that man who was now part of me, that man on TV, that man whose example set ablaze in me the ardency to offer something meaningful to others so that my life would not just be a happy one but a purposeful one. Indeed, how could there be a happy life unless it *was* purposeful? I returned to practice the piano and my fingers pounded out on the keys this message *about* black and white, *in* black and white.

I began my journey into adolescence. Here are a few things that stand out: teaching my much younger brother (with a blackboard and some chalk) anything he might be interested in that I was learning, playing street hockey with him down in the unfinished basement, and helping to get things calm in the house by the sound of the music that my fingers shaped on the keyboard as I let my creative juices flow. (I would soon be recruited by Julliard—never to be for reasons I will explain in due course.)

As an elementary school student, I don't really recall school or any homework—just wanting to help my friend Val learn how to read in 2nd grade, as he lived on a boat in the nearby canal. But what is apparent to me from this reflective perspective is that even at the beginning, even before adolescence, I was being inspired by Dr. King, and then was allowing this MLK to teach, to explain, to motivate. The commitment to teaching was starting to form. It was inseparable from what was highest in me.

It was my royal road to healthy relationship—the sacred relationship that the Jewish ethicist Martin Buber (1965) of Hebrew University described as an "I-Thou" conversation at some of the deepest and most delicate (and also most powerful) strata of one being—at the center of one's being, "where the meanings are," as Emily Dickinson wrote. With "dialogical partners" in spiritually intimate dialogue in the classroom, the conversants, through the medium of the curriculum, enter into deep understanding of not just the curriculum but of each other, as a "Thou," not as an "It." Indeed, to treat another as an "It," as an object, is the sum total of what Buber means by immorality. The equation was simple: The world where everything was treated as an object meant immorality. The world where everything was treated as a Thou mean immortality.

Buber does not prescribe strict moral codes of do's and don'ts. But he does demand that we attend reverently to the humanity of the person with whom we are in dialogue. The dialogists honor each other, even when they do not agree, and, ideally, *especially* when they do not agree, for that is the magical point where they may then learn from each other. The gift to create I-Thou classroom environments is, frankly, not given to everyone. But when one *has* been granted the gift, it often begins to appear early in his or her life. The gift was starting to form before my spiritual eyes. I was too young to put it that way, of course, but I felt it with the certainty that the young do that does not require that one put it in words. This is intuition—another indispensable gift of the great teacher. It begins at this age and in this way.

Twenty years later, the gift was to blossom into a commitment, easy to see in me ("Marty is just a *natural* teacher, don't you think?"). To me the call to teach was clear as a French horn announcing a new theme in vast symphonic piece by Mahler. "Here," I felt (indeed, I *knew,* knew through *feeling,* and felt it all the more because I felt it all the more confidently because I *knew* it in my head, clear as a ray from a diamond sun) that teaching was where I would integrate head *and* heart, just as Dr. King brought them together in his speeches and writings.

Two different ways of knowing—the logic of incisive political thinking with the pull and passion of poetry. But was not this precisely what the best teachers do, too? Is not this exactly what makes for a teacher and a term you will never forget, unlike mostly all of the rest of them, which you cannot forget fast enough? For, it was not only races he united but the logic of political theory with the sacred emotions at the core of the ethical heart. Different ways of knowing, brought together in the practices of the best teachers. That was it! It was what Dr. King was calling me to do. It was to become like him. It was to become a teacher—a spiritually vital teacher. For what is spirit if not the marriage of head and heart.

Dr. King was a teacher to a whole nation. MLK. Yes. He, MLK, who shaped me so that I could become MLK in ethical fact, not just a matter of mere initials. In my smaller way, I would strive to become for my class what he had for an entire people. In such teaching, both teacher and student are liberated so that, though the humane curriculum, negotiated with utmost sensitivity, in I-Thou relationship, we could all say at the end of the term: "Free at last! Free at last!" As I sat at my piano, integrating the black and white of the keyboard, the melodies were different but their theme was always the same: Liberation in education. Education as liberation. I had heard the call, and to it I said "Yes" in thunder! I would be a teacher.

Thirty years later, after I had carried my efforts forward as far as it seemed to me then that they could go in that venue, my "time in the trenches" lived and logged, I moved on, after graduate work at Harvard and Boston University and with a newly minted doctorate in hand, I became a professor of education at what was then the largest college of education in the U.S.— Brigham Young University. How I wound up at that university as a New York Jew is a tale that I will unfold for you as we journey on, especially in the "Postscript" chapter, which the reader of this book, who wishes to know more about the author might turn to sooner rather than later. In it I share with you not only my journey as a bisexual man but as (for a season in my life) a Latter Day Saint, and what this tension wrought in my life, and how it was all part and parcel of my calling as a teacher.

In working with my colleague at BYU at the time, Clifford Mayes, another Jewish-Christian academic in the heart of Mormondom at the time (he went on to become Roman Catholic), and finally collaborating with him on a book, I grew more deeply to understand his idea of "*integral teaching*" and that it answered beautifully to my pedagogical ideas as well (Mayes 2019) involving all of oneself, every aspect from the simply physical to the sublimely spiritual, integral teaching is not for the faint of heart. It is for those who cannot deny their heart.

Now, however, decades later, I am learning the truth of the maxim that often, and more and more often as one ages, applies to the person who has heard the calling and mustered up in himself "the courage to teach" (Palmer 1998). For, one must find this courage in oneself if one is going to fight for humane, integral teaching in school and university venues that are increasingly falling under the grind of the corporatist fist of the military-industrial complex's agenda for education.

For, American education has become largely a matter of standardized education. This is enormously dispiriting to the ethical teacher, one who feels "called" to teach; for, she sinks under a job that has less and less to do with children and more and more to do with legal requirements. She finds that "the spirit may indeed be willing but the flesh is not able" (*Matthew* 26: 41).

But that is also farther down the road, when we discuss the phenomenon of teacher burnout and what can be done about it to "reclaim the fire" of becoming a teacher (Mayes, Grandstaff, and Fidyk 2019).

For now, what I am asking you to see, to become aware of, even (ideally) to take in and take on, is that teaching occurs in broad shifts, almost like tectonic plates, over the years. I wish to help you see—even to become comfortable with—the developmental stages of a teaching career. The desire to teach leads to becoming prepared to teach, of course. And once that happens, one is raring to go, filled with the excitement of a core commitment to young people and democracy on the cusp of being fulfilled. What Freud called "the reality principle" then sets in after a while. For, this is hauntingly, at times exasperatingly complex work.

Frustration often then descends upon the teacher, the weight of his work on his shoulders, like Aeneas carrying his aged father on his back out of their burning city. This weight includes increasingly standardized instruction; high stakes assessment (Berliner and Biddle 2005); symbolic and actual surveillance of the classroom (Bernstein 2006); lots of public statements, usually by a politician eager to garner votes by trashing teachers; ethnic and socioeconomic variations and conflicts within the culture of the school itself; and limited funding coupled with unrealistic expectations of schools, and so on. Is it any surprise that within five years of deep questioning about whether this role is really for them, half of the teachers have left schooling? I wish this pedagogical autobiography to be both a warning about this but to be conveying in an essentially hopeful manner how to renew the vision and the vocation.

What I wish to lay out as I ponder this journey is that the reader do the same, taking on board this work of looking more deeply at what it took to arrive at this point in one's life while discovering the connections to be found between the evolution of the career and that of the containing life journey that developed from the time one was the age of one's current students to the present moment in which one finds oneself, trying at the same time not to lose himself and his sense of calling.

As an adolescent, I was taught by many competent teachers but only one outstanding teacher. She taught English. In my reflectivity on what has shaped me into the teacher that I am, I see that it was by admiring her example of what it meant to teach and how best to do so, I also internalized that image of her in what we might call "the archetype of the good teacher." Majoring in history at Princeton, I would be blessed with memorable professors in that field as well as others whose examples I also loved and whose approach to teaching I also absorbed and placed in the internal archetypal "the good teacher." So, the first point of reference was that my commitment to teach was laid by my intuitive desire to empower my brother, followed ten years later by watching professionals offer me their best—unraveling the material, making insightful connections across the historical landscape, and performing their theatre so well as to cause me to catch the fever.

But learning does not occur in a cultural vacuum. What counts as "knowledge" and what are the best ways to put that knowledge to work are often largely cultural matters. I excelled in school. I wound up going to some of the most sought-after universities in the nation. I would ultimately be granted a doctorate from one of them. But what did all of that mean if I wound being "just a teacher"? To my 3rd-generation Jewish American parents, introducing me as "my son Martin, the doctor!" or "my son Martin, the lawyer" would justify all the toil that my school and university years had entailed. But "my son Martin, the high school teacher"? No. That would never do. Succeeding at learning was fine, but only if . . . "Only if what?" you ask? The answer is simple. Only if my conquests in school led to me "getting a job in one of those skyscrapers that we could see on the western horizon." For that would prove success—and validate the efforts of my Jewish parent's cultural cohort, 2nd and 3rd generation Jewish-Americans, and, as if arranged to complete the stereotype, with my grandparents coming from either Brooklyn or the Bronx. In short, I left school and headed off to college equipped with great aspirations but saddled by grinding neuroses. And here is a secret that parents would do well to meditate on: the extremely high-achieving student may be as much of an educational problem as a low-achieving one. It is called "learning for love" instead of the "love of learning" (Eckstein and Motto 1968).

Their narratives would (they felt) be brought to a successful conclusion only if I graduated from a prestigious law school or medical school. In a sense, therefore, when it came to my entire educational life and what was to come of it, I *had no narrative.* Or rather, my narrative boiled down simply to this: "Justify your ancestor's narrative of suffering by becoming what they valorized. Forget where your gifts are leading you and giving you the deepest pleasure and the highest purpose. Slay who you are. Deny your own reality. Turn your back on a divine calling to teach. Instead, become something you loathe in order to redeem your family's narrative. Your *truth* is to live a lie. Their heaven must be built on your hell." This is what D.W. Winnciott, the post-Freudian theoretician and child psychiatrist called "living as a false self" (1992). I was the poster child of that problem.

So here is another pedagogical gem I offer you, one that was formed in the deep earth of my own experience: When you see a child sitting in front of you at her desk, realize that sitting with her is a long string of parents and grandparents and great grandparents. Even if we only go back 20 generations, each person has close to a million direct grandparents. They are all sitting in a spiritual space around your student. All of them have written a line in the grand narrative of "What education means to our family." Your student has not only inherited those grandparents' DNA. She has inherited their narrative about education. And to make matters even more daunting, realize that you have as many such narratives in your classroom as you have students. How important it is to see to it that each student has as affirming, expansive, and psychospiritually rich experience in the classroom. Twenty million people are depending on it!

And so, this history major was supposed to go to law school. Thus, the honest conversation was impossible to begin—that I *might* want to teach. That is, making less money than a garbage man. Culturally, I was dead in the water (although I would find out a few years later that I had a grandmother secretly rooting for me). It would take a couple of extraordinary conversations with a respected woman in the community, a classmate's mother, to invite me to "go for it."

Of course, this leads me to approach the question of why I wanted to teach that particular age group: secondary school adolescents. Why them?

Easy. My life just ten miles southeast of the craven world of Trump, just 20 miles southeast of midtown Manhattan. It was, to me, a world of immorality. "Sex, drugs, rock and roll" was our mantra. "Do whatever you want, just don't get caught, and you'll be fine" was the parents.' Deep within me, I knew there had to be more to life. To be sure, and to this day, I am one of only several of my peers who felt that way . . . and who saw fit to leave that ethically-mired matrix to incorporate more spirituality into their life narratives—even if it meant making less money than a garbage man!

The point is just this: My own adolescence was fraught with achievement. In a sense, it was rotten with success. I am referring here to the never-ending cycle of success which begot even harder efforts, which triggered more success—but always living in the anxiety that perhaps the next time around I wouldn't be so successful. What would that mean? Would it mean that I was no longer lovable? Would my teachers then reject me if I did not always get the highest scores? And even more chillingly, horrifyingly, was the question of whether my parents would still love me.

And to top it all off was the fact that I had a complete lack of any sense of what I was *really* striving to learn, for I was not learning anything for its own sake, or for *my* own sake; I was not learning out of any intrinsic passion beating within me for the subject matter. No. Like Pinocchio, I was not a *real* human boy. I was more like a performing monkey. I was learning tricks just to get the positive reward of tasty little tidbits of their love with each new high test score. I was not a son. I was an amazing pet.

The well-known researchers of the 1960's in the deep psychological dimensions of teaching and learning, Ekstein and Motto, would capture the syndrome brilliantly in the title of their (1969) book, *From Learning for Love to Love of Learning.* The first part of that title—that was me! The last part is what I would strive a lifetime to discover.

It is wise as a teacher to be just as concerned about the student who is always the best at everything in class as it is about the student who is always struggling with everything. Indeed, the latter student's problems may point simply to cognitive issues that can be relatively straightforwardly addressed. But the former student's successes may point to deep psychological issues regarding emotional abandonment and conditional love that leave him neurotically straining to get 100% on everything. This typically leads to depression, anxiety; to a sense of living as a "false self" (Winnicott 1992); to substance abuse, and even to suicide. Which problem is greater?

I submit that in many cases it may be the student who is slavishly craving for love that he is not getting anywhere but in his academic brilliance than in the student who has some manageable cognitive problems, perhaps, but is being lavished with love at home by parents whose only wish is that their child be happy and know that he is accepted and even cherished. As a teacher, I will choose the second student's problems as much more manageable than the first student's agonizing contradictions.

As my budding career unfolded—with my becoming a high school teacher/coach/adviser/mentor in south Florida—it slowly became apparent that what I was doing was pouring my energies into the lives of the age group that had been the toughest in my own life—16–18 years old. If I could save them, perhaps I could symbolically save myself, which, of course, was not realistic but what does that matter to the subconscious mind, for which everything is always going on at the same time in the present? The idea that time is a metaphysical absolute in a steady stream forward in a perfect line in absolute increments that are always the same, is a rational product of the conscious mind. It is what Newton meant when he said that "Time flows equably of itself."

But since Einstein in physics and Freud in psychology, we know that there are many kinds of time, not only Newtonian time. The Newtonian definition and experience of time are what is called "secondary processes." But it is not in *secondary processes* that our thoughts originate. Rather, it is in the timeless and endlessly creative dynamic of the personal subconscious and collective unconscious—that is where all of our thought processes begin with. These are the *primary processes*. And they are not always pretty. The poet William Butler Yeats described it as "the foul rag and bone shop of the heart." Of course, primary processes also contain some of our highest ideals and most beautiful impulses. In any case, they come before secondary, conscious thought. So we call them "primary processes."

It has become very clear in depth-psychology that the subconscious underlies and can undermine the conscious mind. This is why we must give primary processes profound attention in our pedagogies. Thus, here, even in looking at something apparently as straightforward as the question of why I choose to teach children of a certain age, the complete answer to that could never be just rational speculation but would have to include all sorts of images, moment, triumphs, and tragedies that were so central to why I taught the age group that I did.

My mantra, during those years in Dade County, was "Save them from the ravages of MTV . . . and cocaine." I had no idea what they did on weekends. They actually sought to protect *me* from going anywhere I could get into any trouble. And so, Coral Gables, South Beach and even Coconut Grove were off-limits!

Interesting how these teenagers (and yes, it is most certainly the other, larger half of the paycheck to enjoy strong friendships with many of them more than 30 years later) sought to keep me above board—as they told me they needed me to remain innocent so that could keep coming back to me, knowing I would be there, as "Kokol" to them, that they might confess their sins. They hinted at these sins in their own ways, feeling that I was not tarnished, bruised or taken out by the craziness of 1980s Miami. As they confessed to me, I knew two things.

First, that what I was wrestling with was not a sin but a question of sexual identity, mostly, or at least largely, given at birth, and what God had implanted could not be a sin. More of this as this tale continues to a culminating vision in a Sacred Grove, where I found liberation, indeed, from this unnecessary shame, shame that could result in a teen's self-destruction, and *that* I would not allow. Second, I knew that I was, in this sense, their priest after soccer practice, and during lunchtime, a bit of their therapist. Not a bad calling for a late-20-something—to find meaning in this archetypal image! Teacher as philosopher would have to await another era when I would be more fully grounded in the cognitive domain as I already was in the physical and emotional worlds.

And here we see a theme that will emerge and play a large role throughout this account—namely, that one's larger life-existential narrative is not separable from one's narrative of oneself as a teacher, not if one's sense of calling as a teacher is a deeply ethical one that imbricates, and is imbricated by, the great themes, struggles, impulses, commitments, and, yes, even ambiguities that make up life in the first place. To say I am a teacher is in many vital ways tantamount to simply saying "I am." The teacher brings who he is to the classroom. He teaches character in his example as much as he teaches curricular objectives in his pedagogy. One's deepest and highest feelings about life and one's deepest and highest for oneself as a teacher: Could they ever be separated? No! Not if one feels he has been called by something Divine to do something that matters to that divinity: To teach!

The commitment to these emerging young adults was the culmination of gaining the education and the experiences I would need to be of help—to go through my own pain, battle my own demons, question my very efforts—so that I might have legitimacy for their adolescence 10 to 15 years after my own had come and gone—although the point that it never really goes is what I am driving at here. And I am further suggesting that one who is called to teach may also be being called to heal himself by helping to heal others at what was a particularly problematic phase of his own lifespan development. The unfolding of my religious life at this stage of my evolution as both a teacher and a soul is a good case-in-point here. For, what happened next was a revealing shift in this regard, as I would no longer find commitment to the zip code in which I worked, even to the age group I was teaching in the first chapter of my career, as my primary motivation.

The shift began as a recognition that it would be towards getting back into learning as an academic discipline, not just a daily classroom practice. I would head north to Cambridge/Boston for two rounds at graduate work resulting in the doctorate so that my teaching (not even knowing where this would all lead me) would be rekindled, refocused, reframed in terms that included but went beyond my commitment to a particular classroom in a particular locale with particular students. Parallelly, my new sense of my calling of a teacher would still embrace but also transcend my attendance once per week at a house of worship. This was not enough. It did not suffice. Faith, to be full, to be generous and nurturing of not only oneself but others, had to fructify in even more extensive and intensive action in the world.

In brief, I was learning, in a very up-close and personal way, not just as a matter of intellectual assent, that faith to be great—indeed, to be complete— had to go beyond the comfort of doctrinal "certitude," a feature of faith at an adolescent phase of development, according to James Fowler (1981) in his classic study of maturing in one's spiritual life—*Stages of Faith.* It had to blossom beyond the pleasant but still partial and "local" little patch of the religious commitment of a particular faith-community with which one identi- fied (really, with which one's *ego* identified).

Faith, I was discovering—in precisely the same moments and motions and in much the same ways as my sense of calling as a teacher was now expand- ing way beyond its early, local origins—had to blossom beyond its ultimately tiny little garden-of-origin and flower into service to all others, regardless of their religious commitments or lack of them, regardless of their sexual identity, regardless of their putative "promise" doing things that a corporate capitalist society might laud but that were death to the soul for many of us. This more all-inclusive and culturally-sensitive form of faith and teaching was, again according to Fowler, a feature of more mature faith and comprises what Mayes characterizes as "teaching in the spirit" (2020). I was in my faith life, then, also personally resolving an issue of the age group that I taught. My life-narrative in general and my pedagogical narrative, in particular, were so intricately interwoven—like the multicolored lines of thread on a Navajo tapestry—that one could not say where one definitively stopped and the other started.

SPIRITUAL DEVELOPMENT IN AND
FOR THE CLASSROOM

What did this mean for me as a teacher? It meant that I would be experientially able to help my students resolve issues at their developmental stage—not because I had learned about those issues in a developmental psychology class but because I was resolving them—myself both the teacher and the student, and my own heart the curriculum—in the classroom of my soul. Mind you, this is *not* to say I would start bringing my own spiritual processes and perspectives into the classroom. And naturally, we would talk about spiritual matters explicitly in the curriculum only where they were relevant to the curriculum. Nor would I advocate my own but would serve instead as an honest broker in classroom discussions where students expressed their own in subtle ways, to be sure, and consistent with the prohibition of the discussion of religion in ways that did not relate to the curriculum and, moreover, of religious advocacy of any sort in the public school classroom.

That was the law and I would, of course, happily abide by its wisdom regarding the division of church and state. But I could do this. My training in American history showed me both the wisdom of those First Amendment guide rails in the classroom which I could and would easily follow. At the same time, I would, by example as well as by instruction, help my students grasp that the best reality—at least, the best reality for each one of them as a unique existential being—might not fit into the supermarket-shelf precise sections that consensual reality valued above all else, and certainly valued above the soul of the individual student. As a teacher, I would valorize those souls.

What I did not know at the time is that, in all of these recognitions and metamorphoses, I was following the royal road to discovering in myself (and later would be able to help my students discover) a flexible and capacious faith so that, even beyond the reinvesting in myself as an individual (important as that was) I was finding that the features of my faith were evolving into the lineaments of what Jung would call a fully *integral,* quite *holistic* form of religious vision. And it was one that was of a piece with my overall psychospiritual development. I stress again, therefore, my fundamental insistence that, for the teacher who has heard the spiritual call to teach, her evolution as a teacher simply cannot be seen as separate from the evolution of her core, psychospiritual "Self," as Jung put it, capitalizing the word to indicate that it was the eternal individual who was evolving here, not just the little, temporal ego.

To forge a commitment as a teacher, one must soon recognize that, as Parker Palmer reminded all of us in his seminal work *The Courage to Teach* (1998) we do not, finally, teach what we know, although such teaching is important. But in the last analysis, and much more significantly and durably in terms of our effect on our students, we teach who we are. I might add that, across a career, we might even share with our students what we are becoming—and the journey into deeper realms of relating to a classroom—always, of course, maintaining appropriate emotional boundaries; this is often a tricky balancing act with a class and one that some teachers would avoid on principle. That is understandable. But for some of us, a certain degree of this kind of emotional interaction is a crucial part of the pedagogical process. To be sure, however, great care must be taken.

Stepping up into higher education, I found that my work as symbolically a priest and sometimes therapist had to open up to additional roles. I found myself retooling with a new discipline (Secondary Education), focusing not so much on the student, but on teaching as the object of a whole field of academic inquiry. It provided a period of a sort of blessed detachment and cool objectivity away from what can be the emotional roller-coaster of the teacher in the thick of her student's and her own emotional life every day in the psychodynamic complexity of the classroom—what Irene Salzberger-Wittenberg has elegantly captured in the title of her study *The Emotional Experience of Teaching and Learning* (1989).

As I proceeded into the world of higher education, where I would teach, supervise, administrate and research/write/publish, I didn't realize that the commitment was no longer only to teaching as such although one may not lose that commitment and remain a spiritually authentic researcher into educational issues, which, alas, is too often the case in corporatized colleges of education these days (Cremin 1988). No. The commitment now magnified itself to education as the focus of scholarly inquiry from psychological, sociological, historical and philosophical points of view. I would continue to teach, but now it would be to educate undergraduate and graduate students largely through my scholarly writing and university lectures. As somewhat of an extravert, this would be a relatively difficult assignment, but the discipline was healthy for me.

My commitment was now not just to a job, although that commitment is undoubtedly a very noble one, but to a more prestigious profession—with all of the personal advantages and also temptations that come with such a bump-up in status. This, again, is where reflectivity on one's evolution as a teacher (such as the very one I am engaged in in writing this chapter, in fact!) is so useful in helping the teacher clarify himself to himself. He thereby is more able to explore the positive possibilities in his enhanced role as teacher and the inner dynamics that go along with that advancement. In this way he may more nimbly avoid the dangers professional advancement can entail. This was important to me also because I taught not only undergraduates but occasionally graduate students as well, and for not a few of them, it is the added prestige and buffed up paycheck that matter the most.

Slowly, almost imperceptibly, I found that my career at the university was also becoming a calling, whereas initially I had gone back to the university only to prepare myself to be of ever greater service in the public schools. And this was not, as an outside observer at the time may have understandably but erroneously surmised, just because I had become a Latter Day Saint; that is, a Mormon, in an effort to combine the good works of my Jewish roots with the grace of God in my Christian faith. Nor was it just because I had moved to Salt Lake City to find a wife (just one, thank you!). And it was not just because my impressions when I taught were tinged with something larger than mere thought, subtler than the deepest emotion. These were all part of receiving the call to teach, it is true.

No. This was coming from "something far more deeply interfused" as Wordsworth put it in *The Prelude* in his recognition of his calling as poet as coming from another realm of existence—or rather, from another existence, one that was transfiguring the one I had more or less always known. And it came of its own, in sovereign power that I did not invent, nor could I have done so if I had tried. On the medieval stone tower that Jung built to spend many hours in solitude as he worked out his view of the psyche as a form of Universal Spirit, is written the Latin motto: "Vocatus atque non vocatus, Deus aderit." "Bidden or unbidden, God will enter." That God was entering my life now in a special way and it was all of a piece with my new sense of calling as a professor.

I knew from the glorious moments that occurred on occasion in a classroom with one's students or, as now in my life as a scholar of education, that there is another force that was engaging all of us in the public school classroom and (all too rarely, but it still happens!) as educational scholars. As teachers and learners (for we all play both roles in many situations in just the course of a day) we were sharing something even more significant than the normal ties that bind. It transcended even the curriculum. The curriculum was the launching pad from which the exploratory space vehicle of the relationship between a teacher and student takes flight. But it is not the flight.

That flight into new space is, to be sure, grounded in the curriculum, and it must constantly be checking back with the mission control of the official curriculum that we examined in the Introduction so that it does not wander into uncharted, maybe even dangerous territory, that the formalized relationship between the teacher and student is meant to guard against. Still, the flight is about the teacher and his students, not mission control—now far away. Always within appropriate bounds, of course, it is nevertheless true that the teacher and students must be the final arbiters of which direction to steer their ship; they, the ultimate navigators determining what planets of knowledge to explore together, on what new heavenly formations they will leave their joint footprints—their shared signature on the parchment of the cosmos.

The fact that most of the students where I had been teaching were also Latter Day Saints brought with it a nexus of social and ecclesiastical connections to my students and their parents, both in church and on the street, that was common in the early 19th century frontier town but very rare today (Ravitch and Vinovskis 1995). Having been a student of history at Princeton, I was living out that bit of American history in my own life.

One thing was for sure. In this newly-understood commitment to education (and to address fully my desire to assist, motivate and inspire those between 16–25)—my work was no longer as a secondary social studies guy. It was far more complex—as I came to understand, now in my 40s, that my own life was strengthened with challenges but also fraught with peril at that age. And so, the calling (which I would come to realize, but really not completely accept until recently) was extended to include not just high school students, but also undergraduates and then master's degree candidates as well. The commitment to education insured that I would make this arc my life's work.

The calling occurred—indeed, it came barreling back with redoubled force—each time I tried to walk away from the profession, in order to try my hand at something far more remunerative. And so, not only once but twice in the next decade, I would find myself studying for the Series 7 exam in order to prepare to trade stocks and bonds, to buy puts and calls and naked puts and even understand straddles. But, it was not to be! No matter how much the ghosts of those skyscrapers from my own adolescence wooed me to enter and ascend, education in one form or another called me back. I had been chosen. And that was that.

Teaching undergraduates at two universities in Utah, I found myself humbler and more compassionate in my work—humbled that I was the newcomer to these zip codes, that I was the newcomer to this religious view; and in some ways, I was quietly learning from my students. Commitment to teaching is laudable. But I found that the greatest source of my happiness was to learn from them and what drove them spiritually. Many of them had already "served" missions for their church for 18 months to 2 years, with the hope that they would teach others what it was they believed. The missionary's function is primarily a pedagogical one. They came to my classroom, as, in a sense and in their own ways, already "seasoned teachers." And so, this experience of teaching them at Brigham Young University followed by Utah Valley University, lasting a total of 10 years, found me not so much teaching others *how* to teach, but helping them understand *why* they would teach in the American public schools and *what* they could offer.

And in case it wasn't clear to me by then that I still had a great deal to learn about myself of a highly intimate nature, the mother of all midlife crises hit just when I thought I was settling into fatherhood (with three daughters, aged 9, 7 and 5). My life's journey would be interrupted by unfinished business.

Like the teen/young adult who is now beginning to see and make the first motions towards resolving the tension between identity and intimacy that typifies this developmental age group, I found I had some work to do along these developmental lines. And it apparently wouldn't wait. But then again, when the two narratives—the existential and the pedagogical—weave up so close together that they form a knot, one cannot wait. One must suffer, reflect, and act. And this is what I would do!

To put it bluntly, not only were my psychospiritual issues surfacing and striving towards resolution during this season of my transformation as a teacher. So were psychosexual ones. I deal with these at much greater length in chapter 2, to which the reader may turn at any time he or she pleases, especially as it might touch on some of their own issues along these lines.

For now, let it be enough to state something that once one bounds onto the new existential grounds that present themselves in attending to one's "calling" as a teacher, one can find oneself not only on Elysium fields but also in some pretty deep and even dangerous zones, sometimes even hellish ones. There are aspects of one's life that need to be faced, held up to the light for close scrutiny, viewed from every angle, polished up or whittled down, and, in short, profoundly *reflected* on and then *acted* on in courage and good faith.

For, the transformation from "work," to calling is a sea-change, whether it happens in a Road-to-Damascus vision in the stroke of a mystical moment or as a gradual plate-tectonic shift in the gradual depths of psychological processes. To transition from work to calling means, by definition, that something is in need of serious retooling, painstaking polishing, and of almost apocalyptic upgrading in this mortal run. Any cracks in the plaster, any fissures in the glass, any mushiness in the foundation upon which calling can be fully realized—this all requires that considerable inner work must go on, even if it means stepping away for a few years, which is what I now did after my decade-long season in academia.

Arriving at the Teacher as Philosopher engenders pain and requires patience. It is the beginning of wisdom; for, it is true, as the Jewish tradition states, that the acquisition of wisdom begins somewhere around age 40. So it was for me. And it didn't come from a book. It came from a broken heart (in my personal life), an overloaded mind (tenure track woes), and a shattered spirit (loss of faith). Fortunately, I lived through it all, a dramatic emergency room experience in which I was a hair's breadth away from a full-on heart attack notwithstanding. The key is to accept loss, apparent failure, even when hope has all but drown in the dark ocean of despair.

Resurfacing in New York City, thanks to family help, I found myself learning something really important in the syllabus of the School of Hard Knocks about this stage of a career—something that it is wise to learn, even if it's at 50—my age then. It is where one comes to before one heads off into the next chapter of life. I knew I had run away from the world I was raised in. That was no secret. "Go West young man" was my high school English teacher's advice—and I had taken it seriously. Look where it had landed me!

So I returned to the Big Apple to teach at another graduate school of education. Who were the graduate students I would now teach at this new assignment? Young men and women (some even in their 40s) who were from the City, not the suburbs like myself. Many were second generation Americans—like my father. Most all of them longed to do a good work for their community. I knew what they wanted.

What I could offer was simply some perspective for having traveled and lived west of the Hudson. And so, the entertainer emerged—as I took them on an I-80 tour, far beyond the bounds of New Jersey. Interactive theatre began here. Indeed, isn't it true, as Seymour Sarason has written, that the best teachers, the most memorable ones, are best and most memorable because they approached "teaching as a performing art" (1999). This is not to say that they use the curriculum as an occasion just to get a few laughs. Nothing could be farther from the truth.

Rather, they present the material in such a way that both the comedy and tragedy, those two masks of Greek Drama, that make up the human condition—and that therefore must infuse the humane curriculum—electrify the classroom as everyone gets a sense of the triumphs and the tragedies of the people, ideas, and places that we are studying. Such a teacher wins a place in our hearts and minds forever. And how could she not? She has made learning real for us and thus made us more real through learning.

To be sure, I needed all the skills in my pedagogical quiver polished and at the ready when a bunch of young men arrived in my classes in the Spring of 2009, fresh from being fired from Wall Street jobs. I knew that I had to make it worth their while to be in the classroom. Normally, I bridle at the cold calculus of any cost-benefit analyses to assess the educational worth of a lesson, a unit, and especially the whole term at a school site. I revolt at the idea (because it is revolting) that our principal criterion in educating our young should be the cash value of educational processes to the child, her parents, and society a large—what is called "human capital theory" in the economics of education and advocated by the likes of Moe and Chubb (2009). It is the kind of approach to what Bowles and Gintis exposed as the hidden agenda of a great deal of "schooling in capitalist America," as they critically called it almost a half-century ago—and it still is true, indeed even more true with each passing year as the division between rich and poor grows more dramatic.

Specifically, rich kids go to rich schools with gorgeous campuses, all the latest technology, a vast assortment of interesting clubs, and the best of America's teaching force. There, they learn the mindset and acquire the skills necessary to move on, with high college-entrance-test scores, to fine universities and get the degrees that ensure—or at least make it highly probable—that they will stay rich. On the other side of the tracks, poor kids go to poor schools, where they have symbolically beaten into them the low expectations society has for them. They learn this every minute they are on campus. They learn it by the architectural bleakness of the physical site, the scarcity of resources in general, a dumbed-down curriculum, transient and inexperienced faculty, and uninvolved parents. And to dispel the false notion that poor people are poor because they don't care about education, we must remember that the poor tax themselves very heavily but the result is only very low-grade schools because their property base is so low, while the rich tax themselves relatively little as a proportion of their income and wind up with gorgeous school facilities with all that is the best and the latest. So yes, it is true that poorer parents tend not to be so involved in their students' school and *want* to be involved but are generally holding down two or three jobs just to make ends meet and don't have time for rich discussions with teachers at parent-teacher conferences about how to prepare Juan or Fatima or Trang to get into Stanford or Yale.

What these kids learn—the "hidden curriculum," to invoke the terms in the Introduction—is a "poverty mindset," which, along with a depleted curriculum, keeps them oppressed while preparing them for low-paying jobs and a hopeless life. In this way, schools do not so much teach kids some abstract thing called "knowledge." It teaches them who they are and where they are destined to go and what kinds and levels of knowledge they need to know to arrive there—"there" being the place where they started out from, namely, their parents' socioeconomic status. Schooling thus "reproduces" the socioeconomic positioning of students, according to McLaren's powerful "Reproduction Theory" (1995).

But I had to put those nice philosophical objections on pause now. For you see, I was teaching these disgruntled business types just one block from Wall Street, a three-minute walk to the statue of George Washington in front of Federal Hall, a two-minute walk from Alexander Hamilton's grave. But these students wanted cash value out of their education and so I adjusted accordingly. Still, taking former university students those same historic sites before, places that they had not even noticed, until I decided that we had the ultimate field trip to take, was absolute heaven for me. For, *that* class was Social Studies Education.

I had given up the high school classroom for the university lectern and this is where it had taken me. Had I betrayed my calling? Had I made an awful mistake? I wondered these things as the adult money-minded students now stared at me with dollar signs in their eyes. I was perplexed, sad, and feeling not a little guilty. For what they were preparing to do was to become teachers. However, for many of them, this was just as a fall-back position, "until the economy improved" and they could get back to the real point: To make money . . . and lots of it.

What was becoming of my "call to teach"? Had I become a defrocked priest of education? Woe seemed to be piling on woe in my professional and spiritual narratives—always so closely interwoven in the life of a "called teacher" and, like any marriage, through bad times as well as good. Alas, it had come to dawn on me from these extraordinarily heterogeneous classes that my efforts were now not just about the "how" of teaching, but of the "why" of teaching.

Techniques and technology were not enough now. For me, my intellectual hunger was heightened with the economy's demise. What was the purpose of school anyway—at least in New York City? Was it to be the profit of the prophets of capitalism? Where was democracy to be found? John Dewey—along with William James one of the greatest of American philosophers in addition to being, beyond any possibility of controversy, its greatest educational philosopher was, no doubt, rolling in his grave seeing his dream of truly democratic education as the salvation of our nation being utterly savaged. I could just imagine him, frothing as he lay in that grave, waiting for his day to come back again, the second coming of an educational messiah, to wreak his fury upon this "education as the practice of social abuse against children," in Block's memorable phrase (2008). And how could we find evidence that would persuade these Wall Street types who had turned to becoming teachers as a fall-back position (hardly that divine sense of calling that is a major theme of this book that I will work out in what follows) that commitment was more important than ever. For, their generation had watched many of their older peers teach for 2–5 years and then go off to graduate school to pick up another profession.

Bottom line: How could I help my adult students to catch the vision of teaching, to take on "commitment," when their hearts were telling them to simply get this stint in grad school on their resume—and until the economy turned around? Whereas Paul had had a vision of the road to Damascus that awakened him to his true calling, his eternal "vocation," I had had an antivision on the road to Wall Street, had fallen into looking at my job as a balance sheet of costs and benefits, was no longer a moral artist for the divine but a performing pet for the monied, or those who had been monied before and desperately wanted to be so again. It was a knotty (and naughty) situation for me. Where was my calling now? Was it not now kind of reprimand and not an inspiration in my life? How could I live like that? Of course, the answer was: I couldn't.

Considering the complexity of the acts of teaching—emotional, political, cultural, and ethical—Mayes writes: "At the center of it all, a teacher and a student, face to face try to teach and learn. It is astonishing that they get anything of educational consequence done in the classroom. But they do. And that is the miracle of it" (Mayes 2019, 128). The students I was working with now demanded results! Very well then. But what counts are "results" in the very best appropriations and definitions of it? If we posit for just a moment that education must by definition yield notable and noticeable results, indeed noteworthy, even truly significant consequences, how would this be shown? How could we as teachers *make manifest* these results? Could our aims to secure a satisfactory outcome for our STEM (Science, Technology, Engineering, and Math) curriculum suggest some leads for similar results in our foreign languages, even for our sports teams? What would that look like? How would we detail such a success? How would we measure it? Would we need a new vocabulary, not just for the matters of the mind—whereby outcomes could be quantified—but also for habits of the heart—whereby inputs would have to be qualified? How would such an offering be secured? Or even acknowledged? Or even written up? If there is one place I have wanted to secure, if there is one area within education that needs to be tackled head on, at this point of the American journey, I would say it is here in this area— "heartful witnessing and authentic assessing"—that I would seek to secure a complete education. What I propose to do at this point is to try to introduce such a model. I will build upon that model throughout this book to construct an array of such interlocking models, along with exploring their parallels in my own theological, emotional, and psychosexual transformations as I do so. Proust meets Dewey in this book, one could say!

What I propose can be introduced by this napkin-sized sketch that I used to address the basic areas of our lives that cry out for development in education and which we must find ways to assess in the student authentically, richly, and qualitatively:

What we do with all of this, how we will make it *real,* is of first importance for teachers and students in the 21st century. The question is: How does education become humane—that is to say, doctrines and technologies in the service of teachers and students, not the other way around—and how will we be confident that we are accomplishing this in the classroom? What are the new kinds of curricula we will have to write, going far beyond the current view of education as mostly just to prepare one for a job? This is important, naturally. But when it becomes the driving purpose of education, democracy goes a glimmering. Dewey made all of this clear in his classic *Democracy and Education* just over one hundred years ago in 1916. Schools must shape complete human beings, for only complete human beings can resist falling prey to demagoguery, on one hand or, on the other hand, being slyly enlisted into covert networks of control (made all the more possible now because of advanced means of surveillance) that dominate the individual spirit to such an extent that, as with the Borg on Star Trek, "Resistance is futile" and the individual relinquishes his status as a member of a democracy and succumbs to being just another node in a technocracy.

None of the high purposes of schools in a democracy can be accomplished without highly competent, deeply compassionate teachers engaged with students in vitally interesting curricula that both draw from the community in which the school is situated and radiate back into it. A marriage of schooling and national purpose in the sacred font of democracy—that was Dewey's dream and I echo it now.

In large measure, I am sharing my experiences to give a face and a name to just one of scores of thousands of teachers who share that dream. As an educational scholar, I am also pleading that we help teachers find the sustaining water of commitment in the deep spiritual wells of their sense of calling. We can do this by practical measures that show teachers our concern for their well-being. These include giving them more released time, funding for professional development, fewer preparations, and smaller classes, and more respect for their venerable role instead of being scapegoats for all of our society's ills. Manifesting our care and respect for teachers through such means as these is absolutely paramount in this age of ever-increasing tensions and contradictions impacting the work of the teacher in the fractiousness of postmodern America. Let us now delve into these complex, interweaving, and compelling topics in greater personal and theoretical detail so that the all teachers, new and old, can consider this tale of an educator and use it, with grace from above and grit in his or her own soul, to be more complete as a teacher and as a human being in these difficult times into which educational specifically and our culture as a whole has fallen. There is hope! And that is what I wish to communicate in ever-increasing measure as you read on.

Over the past few years, one can easily find a multiplicity of articles all pointing to the very obvious situation we now face in this country regarding unhappy teachers that have recently been or are currently on strike (or now even resigning mid-year), a situation that is also compounded by a teacher shortage that has been reported in respected news sources:

America has a teacher shortage, and a new study says it's getting worse.
Washington Post, September 14, 2016

Why America's teacher shortage is going to get worse. NY Post, February
   14, 2018
School's back in session, but many teachers aren't returning. CBS News,
   August 23, 2018
Teacher shortages worsening in majority of US states. The Guardian,
   September 6, 2018

I have found that my professional life is a sine wave between two poles:
an academic inquiry into education as a member of the professoriate, on
one hand, and a secondary school teacher in the schools, on the other hand.
For all the different amplitudes and frequencies that this has entailed in the
trigonometry of my life as a spiritually-called teacher, this creative dialectical
tension remains constant. Thus, my most recent venture into graduate school
teaching coming to what I felt was a natural end and revitalized to "Go West
(again), Middle-Aged Man!," take off the academic robes, put on my jeans,
shirt and tie again, and get back into the secondary school classroom where
my calling began and where it always feels closest to heaven's will for me.

Thus it was that I availed myself of an opportunity to continue teaching
full-time and online. I repositioned my life in a wealthy Rocky Mountain
resort town, after the years teaching and supervising graduate students in New
York City's public schools. Meeting with students on Zoom.us was to be done
when they got home, after 5pm ET. And so, taking up the advice of one of
the most intellectually gifted students I had taught, I visited the HR office of
the local school district, with their one middle school, one high school and
one alternative high school, and applied to become a substitute teacher. And
that was when I found out what commitment might look like within me. For I
would no longer be supervising all over New York City, and nor was I longer
a part of the college's administrative team that was preparing for the upcom-
ing accreditation visit. And so, I had ample time to do something new.

Commitment to a new community is an easy decision. Commitment to a
school district is simple. But, commitment to a student body and their teachers requires just a bit of reflection—not necessarily about whether or not
the students were worth the time and the pay of a substitute teacher—but
whether or not this teacher had the right stuff to make a difference, to fill the
gaps, to offer something worthwhile. Commitment, then, can be considered a
realization of self-worth and an invitation to examine whether I might make
enough of a mark to warrant my time. What type of a mark? Simply that I had
something to offer, even if it was once a month that I might see a particular
student again, or teach the same subject in the same building once again. It
was a new role for me—something, now, of an educational Maverick, a Gun
for Hire, A Paladin, even (to continue my pageant of popular American heroes

of the 1950s and 1960s), a Captain Kirk, going from one site of engagement to another, and thereby gaining a more panoramic view of schools within a district than I had heretofore known.

My years of teaching online would not carry me to the end of a career—something more fundamental was going to occur. It had come time for me to reconnect with adolescents and actually reconvene with this new generation of "judges" who might see what I have to offer—besides something of the new contours, velocities, and teleologies of my energies as a teacher that I had now developed in so many different ways and in such a kaleidoscopic range of educational venues, and (to be frank) the aura of an Ivy League education that my years at Princeton, Claremont, Harvard, and Boston University would lend any resume.

And who can deny the thrill (maybe unspoken, certainly not touted or cultivated by me), but just as certainly basked in by students that *their* high school substitute teacher, *Doctor* Kokol, was from New York, had attended Princeton and Harvard, and had a doctorate from Boston University. Safe to say, this was no typical profile for a teacher in a Rocky Mountain public school. But, now, was there a good work to be done exactly 30 years later—all the complexities, bells and whistles that brought me to this unlikely stretch of America that I had landed in? Would it be worth it? Was I just some exotic sea creature that had washed up on the shore of this classroom, there to die a gasping demise? Or was the trumpeter of resurrection doing his scales just far enough offstage that I couldn't hear them but was about to blast me into new life with some messianic fanfare with the happy apocalypse of a choir just behind him? I was about to be given quite the surprise.

There is something quite interesting that developed those first few months in those three schools. To be sure, I got to be known rather quickly, as I had married a "local," someone whose family was well-known by some in the community of 12,000. I quickly came to notice that my presence in a local supermarket, at the playhouse, or at a church was enough of a connection for the students to see me as a "real" person of the community.

Commitment was easy for me. The payoff was not the $104/day (mind you, I was able to sub at least 2 days/week), but rather the recognition and further curiosity on the part of the students and their parents outside the school building. Of course, this could cut both ways—offering stronger reason for commitment, but also inviting deeper scrutiny. This would most probably play out in any town where anonymity would be practically impossible!

And so once commitment was secured within my own mind and heart, I found myself happily ensconced in a nexus of commitments—commitment to a partner, commitment to the schools where we lived, commitment to the community and its many manifestations and ceremonies, commitment to exploring new modes of teaching—it all came rushing into play. And this evidenced yet again my most central theme in this chapter: the called teacher's professional narrative and his existential narrative are indissolubly bonded. With a calling so complex and so heartfelt, the healthy thing to do (and certainly the ethical thing to do) is not to "pinch pennies." It is, rather, to deepen the offer. What do I mean by this trope? It means that one is now called upon to give of oneself in increasing measure, as if one were a drink offering in Old Testament times. You pour yourself out in the service of the Divine that is calling as manifested in loving dedication to those young people who have been placed in your charge. This does not mean that you do not maintain certain boundaries that are necessary to stay sane. Of course, you must. It does not mean that you do not save the best of your love for your partner and children (if you have them).

As a professor of education, I have seen too many marital problems arise, leading too often to divorce, when, for instance, a teacher becomes a principal. In her office before everyone else at 7 a.m., she is there, in the thick of every battle until the battle on the football or baseball field at the end of the day as she cheers the team on from the sidelines and, making everything neat and tidy in the office before she locks up, starts heading home around 10 p.m., the last car to leave the parking lot. This is too much. Even love, to remain viable—that is, for the person after a while to have anything in her left to give—must know its human boundaries. That is the balancing act that the called teacher and school leader must learn to perform.

Thus, although the called teacher does become a drink offering, there must still be spirits and Spirit left in her cup at the end of the day. A good practical measure of what I mean can be put simply. It is that the work is unhealthy when it comes to mean everything. But it remains healthy if it is simply the case that one no longer measures one's work by its financial value but instead meets the life-giving, energy-generating standard of meaning more to her than any money ever could while, at the same time, her personal life remains intact and of the highest value. The added advantage, of course, is that one has, both at school and at home, a sense of belonging, of doing something good and beautiful, immediate and important. One becomes an instant winner within oneself and the commitment is secured. But, then, what about calling?

It's one thing for an individual to declare to him/herself that the work they are doing has been "given unto them by God." That would make the calling of a teacher seem secure, with the pronouncement of such a statement. But, there must be some sort of tangible backing to reveal that such a work is not only ordained but also deeply appreciated, even noted for its aid for members of the community. And thus, it behooves even the most religious individual to come up with evidence that one's work has been brought forth with such an imprimatur, that one's efforts can be shown to bear a superior seal of approval by some measure.

That measure, that confidence in offering oneself to others as the true reward, is evidenced in the mature and expansive joy that one sees take hold and then grow in one's students' faces. There is even a name drawn from the psychoanalytic literature on education for what one is seeing in one's students. It is called "effectance pleasure" (Cohler 1989, 79). It is the joy that any individual takes in knowing that he can get real things done in the real world, not just dream about them.

For, the fully realized sense of calling is not be found in the clarity of one's own voice holding forth, however eloquently, and no matter how stimulating the lesson might be. Rather, it happens at the moment where the teacher realizes that most all faces have drawn strangely still, and that everyone's focus is sharp, quiet and coming straight on. This is the beauty of the calling, to recognize when connection is being forged at a very significant level. It might last anywhere from 10 seconds on up. Its force can only be measured by a simple metaphor of "walking on sacred ground"—the realization that the class is not just listening to the fascinating words coming forth, but is also feeling and allowing the lines of connection that are being offered to take root in them, one by one, yes, but also collectively as a "community of learners" in a "culture of learning" (Bruner, 1996). For it is then that calling is recognized, with teacher and students now together on a course of deep effectiveness, planting the seeds for future mentoring if wanted, and even hinting at a couple of them awakened to wanting to continue conversations long after the school year, or even the chapter of their adolescence ends.

Calling, then, is not about how secure one can get in the work; it is when this type of connection is built, because one is not engaging only with students' minds, or even with their hearts. For the work of the mind is to secure knowledge. And this has nothing to do with calling. And the work of the heart is to offer understanding. And this is still not to do with calling (but rather a caring, compassionate and even outstanding teacher). It is the work of the soul to introduce wisdom, to tap deep into the very being of the youth, adolescent or emerging young adult. It is this that will be an indicator that one's calling has borne fruit in the psyche and spirit of the student. It cannot be reproduced by cognitive assessment devices, however sophisticated. It is a matter of soul.

This then turns our attention to the education of the teacher, beginning with the years securing license, and my first invitation to look deeply into what was being offered, from child/adolescent development, to multiculturalism to courses in special ed right on into student teaching. All very important in their own right. All foundational for successful entry into the classroom, but this is just the starting point. Within X number of years, mastery of what I call head, heart, social, and management work all must be clearly put into play. But, even with the lane name of "master teacher," I will venture to say that there is more that the teacher needs to know that he is living up to his "calling." It is the realization by not just students, or even administrators, but *by the community itself,* that this particular teacher has a gift that cannot be replicated. For it is special to that particular master teacher, presents itself in those moments when something both dynamic and foundational has become unearthed. Mind you, this calling is not all about arriving at some magical point in one's career—for I have seen teacher's callings come to an end—one reason being that the calling for doing the work for a particular community comes to an end.

But, by and large, the calling of a teacher cannot be quantified, and is only rarely arrived at qualitatively. The way to identify such a level (or rather a depth) of successful pedagogy is to use language of the believer. *Credo!* I believe! "I believe that something rare is being unearthed in this transaction with my student, and I believe that it has eternal worth!"

Nowhere is any of this to be found in the slick certainties and Madison Avenue buzz-phrases that dominate so much of the literature on the professionalization of teaching and teacher education. Look, for example, at the standards of the Council for the Accreditation of Educator Preparation, and their six recommendations, as quality teacher education continues to center upon "professionalization": an ongoing insistence to whip teachers into some kind of level of expertise that would allow observers of the profession to shake their heads in agreement that deadwood, incompetents and burned-outs would be more easily removed.

To be sure, we are continually haunted by the unsightly spectacle of those that need to leave. But, rarely in my 30 years in public higher and secondary education do I find any reference to the beauty of the profession; rather, the focus is on the beast, which is much more the object of public attention, than on those who shine. But this has been the great shell game we as a society play with teaching. How is the shell game played—perpetrated, is more like it—on the teacher. We take all of our social ills, put them in a poisonous basket, and lay them at the feet of the teacher—as if schooling should (or even conceivably could) solve all of society's woes. We thereby avoid looking at our deep social ills in a soberly reflective mood and clarity that would allow us to actually witness our problems and act on them.

Instead, we make teachers the scapegoats. Is teenage pregnancy rampant? It's the schools' fault for not having done a better job in sex education. Is gas getting scarcer and scarcer and more and more expensive? It's the schools' fault for not having produced enough engineers to solve the problem. Is voter turnout growing more and more attenuated each election, fewer and fewer people choosing to exercise their franchise? Civics' teachers have clearly not done an adequate job of educating students into a sense of civic duty! Nowhere in all of this do we look at the macro- and microfailures that pervade and pervert our democracy in every corner, at every step, and on every land-scape in order to accurately identify the myriad sources of these problems? No, let us instead blame the schools!

If we cannot fully engage with the identity of those called to teach, we can at least step away a bit and come to understand *why* we desperately need those called to teach in our midst. For what they offer, beyond being committed to the work, long after the final step offers no additional pay raises through the years heading towards retirement. (Well, that's Idaho for you.)

New metaphors are needed. Here is one that I would offer. "Leaven for the loaf!" Knowledge would be the cognitive ingredient in the bread. Understanding would be the affective ingredient. Flatbread would certainly be edible. But, the delight comes when wisdom is added—the spiritual ingre-dient. The rise comes. Of course, in order to digest properly, water would be needed, and this would come in the form of social ability for the adult to build connections for the child/adolescent/young adult.

From talking with a few hundred student teachers, it does become obvious that teaching is not an interchangeable part in the complete educational pro-cess, obvious that one's calling is not just about subject matter but also about target audience. 2nd grade teachers, even the most talented, do not make for a wonderful high school teacher. We all know that. Nor does a high school teacher, even the most talented, make for a wonderful 2nd-grade teacher. We know that, too.

As I've already mentioned, I am convinced that the calling is often spe-cific to teaching a certain age group at a developmental stage when one encountered particularly perplexing and still persistent problems in one's own lifespan development. In short, it has a lot to do with when we ourselves had singularly difficult times, leaving unfinished business that we can revisit anew, now with greater wisdom that it is possible to impart to our students. Whatever was unfinished in our lifetime, we can now resolve and pass those benefits on to ourselves.

Here I must stress the importance of reflecting on oneself as a teacher (Mayes, Grandstaff, and Fidyk 2019). For without deep reflectivity on these matters, the teacher may well not only not resolve the problem this next go-around at it but may play issues out in inappropriate, even catastrophic ways, with his students. Indeed, it is precisely that kind of reflectivity that I am attempting to model here for teachers. It is not an easy process. It offers abundant rewards, however, in deepening self-knowledge and professional development. Everyone benefits when the teacher reflects deeply on the issues and impulses that led him to teach not only this or that particular sub-ject matter but to teach it to the age group that he has chosen to work with. Teacher self-reflectivity is thus a gift—a gift that gives to everyone, that we might strengthen our own journey by teaching and mentoring others.

Many years ago, I tried to describe my work to many of my ivy-league peers, now safely entrenched in careers on Wall Street, the law or medicine, with an image. I doubt they understood. I reckon they found it strange. I said that, like a gestating mother, I had been captured by the nine-month calendar. It was my lot, I explained, to carry to term each cycle the one hundred or so souls under my care. I did it (I went on, as if my peers were not already either put off or vaguely pitying), to deliver them to their next stage of life.

I must be clear that this metaphor certainly did not hold up with college students, whom I simply had the pleasure of steering through 16-week semesters. But, as a K-12 teacher, regardless of decade (for my work here has been in the '80s and the '10s and now in the '20s), I was well aware that I had the unique privilege of shepherding them, guiding them, and coaching them for the purpose of making it to the next level of growth. My passion, my determination in my entire career has been in the sphere of getting young people to successfully navigate their journey from now 15 to 24, from the rages of the hormones to the completion of the brain functions and whether I was given one slice of that time for one high school assignment or given another slice of that time with college students (along with novice teachers), I *chose* it in both cases. In every case, indeed, I *choose* to be a teacher. It is emotionally central, existentially indispensable and spiritually core to who I am. The teacher must often rest content in this exercise of his agency as it answers to his highest visions and goals in life. For heaven knows that the world will often enough not understand or reward this deeply ethical choice.

I am reminded of the young poet who idolized the great Austrian poet, Rainer Maria von Rilke. He wrote him a long letter, along with a hefty selection of his poems, to beg the great poet to tell him, the young poet, whether he was really meant to be a poet. Rilke (1934) sent the package of poetry back to the young poet unopened, along with a brief note that would later blossom into Rilke's splendid volume *Letters to a Young Poet.*

Rilke's answer to the young poet was simple. "I do not need to see your poetry to know if you are meant to be a poet," Rilke bluntly (but with a deep kindness as well) replied. "Rather, you need to ask yourself a question: 'Can I live without being a poet?' If the answer to that question is 'Yes,' then, young man, you are not meant to be a poet. But if the answer is 'No,' then I can already tell you, without looking at a word that you have written, that, my friend, you are meant to be a poet." And thus it has been with me as a teacher. You are *meant* to be teacher, you are *called* to be a teacher, and you must periodically *reflect* on it all just as I am doing in this chapter only if you cannot live without it. I cannot. And therefore, I am a teacher.

Other lifelong friends have chosen end of life care, doctors who work with terminal patients; even others have gone with beginning of life arrival, doctors and nurses attentive to the act of birth. Still others, have gone with midlife frustrations regarding legal, economic or social matters. I tried three times, each unsuccessfully, to leave teaching for financial reasons, but, within weeks, I came to realize that I was selling myself away, that the value of my work simply did not call for me to abandon it for the pursuit of a larger paycheck. I saw more deeply than I ever had that my original pursuit for happiness in my labors, for meaningfulness and for purposefulness, was right after all. And that it was only a matter of time before I called myself back to the classroom. Or perhaps my being called back was not primarily my doing.

Perhaps it was Divine Will that was doing this, which I was only partially correctly interpreting as my own. Whatever it was, it was irresistible. It was like being called as a shaman in First Nation cultures. It is a hard calling and supremely difficult work. Many who are called attempt to resist the calling, leave their role as shaman, become just ordinary members of the society. But that does not last for long. The shaman must return to the shaman's role or else he becomes very ill until he does. Similarly, my soul was uneasy, even distressed, until some will—God's, my own, or (most likely) both directed my footsteps back into the classroom. Only there was I happy for only there was I filling the destined measure of my existence.

What was most attractive for me regarding this work? Can it be encapsulated by Sidney Poitier's final scene in *To Sir With Love* in 1968, where he rips up the offer from an engineering firm, after a close encounter with a couple of frolicking future students? For this was my first encounter with calling. Or would I turn, for absolute security to the big screen once again with Robin Williams, the sage on the stage, in *Dead Poets Society* in 1989 and, as a guide on the side, in *Good Will Hunting* in 1997.

What I have learned to be my *life work* (and, at the same time, what I have always *known* to be my life's work) is that I see adolescents and emerging young adults as ends, not as means to other ends—someone else's agenda for the child, not the child's soul's agenda for itself, divinely bestowed and therefore inherently good. These are the stakes, and they are very high.

For, when the child becomes an object, an *It,* in Buber's terms introduced above, then we sin against the child, and, in sinning against the child, betray our better angel and sin against ourselves. And *that* is the essence (I will not beat around the bush) of sin. Only when we see and treat the student as a *Thou,* a fully engaged human being with herself and others, do we, ourselves, become fully *Thou's,* on the road to divinization. When, instead, we treat the child as an object, then we have the warning of arguably the greatest ethicist of the 20th century to reckon with. Buber wrote: "The continuing growing world of It overruns [a person] and robs him of the reality of his own I, till the incubus over him and the ghost within him whisper to one another the confession of their non-salvation" (1965, p. 46). Herein lies the root of great teaching, which, we find upon examining it closely, is nothing other than the heart of morality itself.

WHAT FOLLOWS FROM ALL OF THIS?

The first lesson to be born in mind in our gadget-engorged culture is that technology must be a means only. Even the official curriculum must only be a way to reserve and enrich context. Even instructional strategies matter only insofar as they blessedly entice the student to open up so that student and teacher might connect. The moral is simple, as most great thoughts are. It is simply that human connection must remain front and center. All else is secondary to that lustrous, looming ethical fact.

There is one more piece of the puzzle I wish to mention before we sweep past the notion of calling—and that is the power, the energy, the intelligence that would be requisite for any teacher to utilize their calling for something substantial. What might the fruit of a calling look like, below the evidence of being one of a school's treasures? What might the fuel be to gain success in a calling? I can only remind the reader of Dana Zohar's work out of England right around the turn of the millennium—her book called SQ, which seemed to offer a goldmine, but which, sadly, I did not see catching on in the U.S. The field of spiritual intelligence was about to be born, and it was coming perhaps from one intellectually popular source—Steve Covey's (1989) *Seven Habits of Highly Effective People*—a must-read now for over 30 years. But, it was his eighth habit that somehow didn't catch on, at least beyond the Wasatch Front of Utah. The habit—spiritual intelligence—was, he wrote, "the central and most fundamental of all the intelligences, because it becomes the source of guidance for the others." The subtitle was clear: "from effectiveness to greatness." I loved that clarion call. I lived by it.

Now almost 25 years old, it would appear that the dominance of Google right around then brushed this hugely important find to the side. Spiritual intelligence would become the work of the Dalai Lama. And teaching as calling would slowly recede into the politics of education, with the post-Vietnam generation of teachers firmly in place, with the 2008 recession well on its way to freezing and cutting teacher's pay, and with the slow but steady erosion of seasoned teachers beginning to leave the profession. Indeed, just recently, it was noted that the connection between teaching and calling needs to be sharply reexamined.

Had it not been for all the years in the driver's seat of *No Child Left Behind* (or *No Child Left Breathing* as teachers wryly referred to it in faculty lunch rooms across the nation), SI might very well have pushed education to the next level of federal government scrutiny and funding. whereby the ethos of urban culture—very much under the sway of left-brained, mechanistic approaches to education (and, indeed, to just about everything other than rural, agrarian culture) insists on the right answer. Calling is about as far away from left-brained measurement as can be imagined.

True, we may be seeing some vague possibility forming on our educational horizon for a balance of mathematical /technological ways of thinking with more poetic and intuitive ways of processing experience in mention of the importance of social/emotional learning in public talk about the goals of education these days. But it would be unwise to be swept away with too much hope in such talk. It is still very much on the margins of policies that govern actual practice in the classroom. And even when social/emotional learning does show up in the curriculum, it is still quite secondary, even tertiary. It is a nice afterthought at most in the few classrooms where it even makes the ghost of an appearance. The Jungian psychologist and educational theorist Clifford Mayes is emphatic and detailed in analyzing this problem.

[S]tatistical approaches to psyche, the main means of prediction and control of the individual, are especially antithetical to the spirit of psychology and education since they are antithetical to the spirit of man. . . . Under the influence of scientific assumptions, not only the psyche but the individual man, and, indeed, all individual events whatsoever, suffer a leveling down and a process of blurring that distorts the picture of reality into a conceptual average. State policy decides what should be taught and studied. Statistical, norm-referenced, standardized approaches to education strip the student of her identity, unmask the State as not an instrument of democracy at the local level but a usurper and distorter of her nation's foundational stories at the federal level, and, worst of all, they turn the sky slate-gray and mute for those who now feel alienated from heaven by the excessively secularizing, stealthily encroaching State. In 1961, President Eisenhower in his final address to the nation warned that the growth of a "military-industrial complex" was beginning to pose a clear and present danger to American democracy. In 1988, Lawrence Cremin, the Dean of American *educational* history, went President Eisenhower one better and said that it was the newly emerging military-industrial-*educational* complex that now constituted the threat. Colleges of education have tripped over themselves running towards ever-bigger grants to research ever-more efficient means of training teachers to train children to become obedient and efficient "worker-citizens" through the instrumentalities of standardized education—the dystopian assault on democracy through (mis)education. Dewey is turning in his grave. (Mayes 2020, 129)

The question continues to be "how do we define professionalism" that avoids the business-model of education that sees students (God help us all!) as "human capital" to be increased, and teachers as mere functionaries in bringing this Orwellian future to pass. How could we possibly make room for something like "the teacher's sense of calling" in the mechanist ethos of standardization that is coming to bestride the world like Shakespeare's Colossus?

We do it by very human, situational, and interactive means. We do it by observing the teacher's commitment to students, which can, for instance, be sensed in the amount of time the teacher spends assisting with extracurricular activities. It shines forth in the creativity of classroom walls. Another possible means of getting a solid fix on a teacher's calling might be in the world of mentorship—her willingness to take on the role of a master teacher to be assigned to the rookie or novice teacher for the express purpose of not only assisting with curriculum development, instructional strategy, local school culture and personal development—but also to offer something that we have really neglected for this work, that being an adult relationship in a sea of childhood or adolescence. If there is one thing that I have seen lacking in my 38-year career, it is the notion of camaraderie for the express purpose of support.

What would it take for someone designated the "master teacher"—not just because of X number of years in the field, and even combined with X number of credits beyond the bachelors or even master's degree—to become a "master mentor"? How could we train such a treasure for the school? How might we offer an education—probably in the schools of education, but possibly in a philosophy class—that would invite the soon-to-be master teacher an opportunity to demonstrate what it means to be called, not only for him/herself, but especially for the express purpose of successful mentorship?

Now, suddenly, we have arrived at the precipice whereby we truly need to take on the task of defining a "teacher ladder" to indicate how far up she has moved towards becoming this crowning personage in a department: a master teacher and a master mentor? This is a crucial concern in teacher development—a perpetually looming question that not only goes unanswered but is all too rarely asked. I am mentioning it—indeed, I am insisting on it—so that mentoring can finally secure its rightful place in the work of master teachers, and so that "calling" can finally be included in the developmental stages of a teaching career. This is something I have pondered and co-authored about over 30 years ago with my doctoral adviser, Kevin Ryan, at Boston University. For now, allow me to mention a few of the most salient components of this question of how to define and how to promote the growth of the truly humane teacher, called to serve through mentoring.

To begin with, I will make the perhaps unorthodox claim that "teacher professionalism" is really linked to enhancing one's student's emotional and spiritual quotient (and not just the cognitive). Chinese President Xi Jinping has gone on record and pointed out the primary importance of EQ as "important for adapting to society (although it should be used together with professional knowledge)." Why do I say that they are linked? Because I will venture to assert that cognitive downloading is no longer the critical offering of a teacher. Google, Siri, and Alexa have effectively ousted that as the primary drive in many of the traditional secondary school matters, at least as far as the students are concerned. And so, with the continued realization that these Smartphones have transformed this current Generation Z away from human interaction and towards technology, it becomes even that much more important that what matters most in the classroom, what the teacher can do to offset this imbalance, what the master teacher can offer to the teen students *and* the 20-something teachers, is to *reconnect emotionally.* And to introduce the fundamental issues, the driving questions that are screaming for attention in this first quarter of the century: The need for the spiritual, which is quite simply to say: our instinct to seek out and solve matters larger than ourselves, and to do so in the service of our fellow human beings.

Relationship is the critical ingredient that exists in a successful school—the *sine qua non* of its success. One reads about it all the time—how private schools brag about their community; and one understands, if only intuitively, what it is for the gems of teachers that stay in a welcoming community for a career. The quality, even the existence of mentoring (and again, this is not to be confused with the impersonal metrics that are usually used to gauge professional evaluation) between administrator and teacher is the cornerstone of what type of community is being built in each and every school. Whether the school is built on the factory model, meant to churn out products, or whether the school is built on the community model, meant to develop meaningful relationships—*that,*" as Hamlet would say, "is the question." To put it bluntly, how much of school is meant to contribute to capitalism's wants? How much of school is meant to contribute to democracy's needs? And how much of school's efforts are meant to contribute to individual happiness?

We have been seeking such a balance at almost every turn since the rise of the American public school about 150 years ago (Tyack 1974). The imperative for K–12 education for 2020 is to reconcile, even to create a synergistic harmony between these fundamental needs: intellectual growth with maturing relationships both interpersonal *and* intrapersonal (thank you, Howard Gardner), where the intuitive *and* the logical are welcomed (Gardner 1983). And ultimately, where the rational, the emotional and the spiritual can be found—somewhere along the X axis where man and machine are viewed, somewhere along the Y axis where humanity and divinity are pondered. It is then, and *only* then, that commitment can be assessed and calling can be ascertained.

Of course, in the end, this might be simply too much of a stretch for where we are in our American educational journey. I realize that all this might become the province of the charter schools constructed and yet to be built. Head, heart and spirit must all dance together in concert. Of course, many might take the third element—spirit—and house it simply in the primary religious tradition of the community.

But, before we give up, might I offer this: First, using the head, the teacher motivates, the student performs; the result is achievement, satisfying the needs of the state. Second, using the heart, the teacher inspires, the student aspires; the result is dream construction, satisfying the wants of the individual. The intermediate problem here: unlocked precision is crushing; unbridled passion is destructive. The head *must* work in tandem with the heart. Commitment is the satisfaction that these two are now fastened to each other.

If the head and heart work together with the spirit (or, to look at it another way, one's deepest intuition), the calling is the joy that all three are now favorably stretching each other. As Parker Palmer said: We don't teach what we know. We teach who we are. Indeed, in the end, I believe we must always be teaching what we are becoming. If we can arrive at this fortuitous synthesis, we are really sharing our journey in the space between our humanity and our divinity. Commitment along with calling now becomes secure.

Chapter 2

To Be Gifted and Queer

An Educative Journey

GIFTED AND QUEER

My piano teacher was right. So was my mother. As a researcher. As a teacher. As a performer. And, for starters, as a student. I guess it has been quite difficult to want to learn more about myself. It has always been more fascinating to learn about others—and in keeping a distance from them so as to not really be a part of the discovery, the story. For, in the face of the potentially horrible cost to the child, as we saw in chapter 1. This cost is heightened by the realization (which alone constitutes wisdom) that we are all fairly clueless in the face of the Great Mystery of things.

Please understand that I use this term, "gifted," with that important caveat always before me. I am also not only aware of but deeply shaped by Gardner's (1983) idea of multiple intelligences. Many people are gifted in many ways. To understand my educational and existential journey, I do so, realizing also my many shortcomings where others demonstrate a soaring intelligence. And moreover, in light of the inscrutable and immeasurable intelligence of the divine, we are all less than minuscule.

Thus, although reluctantly, I must speak of my own constellations of gifts in order to mine the story of their development, and the challenges to their development, that I hope the reader will make her or his own, in their own terms, and in a way that honors the cross-fertilization of one's overarching existential narrative with one's educational narrative. To make it clear how that synergy has worked and failed in my own life will, I hope, help others bring the two into creative alignment in their own lives. That is, in a sense, the guiding principle of this study. Thus, reluctantly but necessarily, I speak of my "gifts" in order to accomplish the purposes of this book.

But first, a few more details about my life. I was born of goodly Jewish parents in the older suburbs of Long Island. I lived close to PS #1 in my village, built in 1930. From the beginning, my life has been overflowing with reminders, both physical and symbolic, of my calling, starting with me as a small boy in the early '60's. The formation of my consciousness, the blessed tumult of the Sixties, and an old (but now torn down) schoolhouse—they were all of a piece for me. Schooling, touching every aspect of the growing child's life, must be seen holistically. And seen holistically, understood as part of one's life narrative; one's narrative of oneself as an existential being cannot be separated from his narrative of himself as an educational being. There is hardly an issue in one's life that does not have some school roots and have some school consequences.

If we take it a step farther—as Mayes (2020) has done in a recent study—and look at life in general as an ongoing process of teaching and learning—of life, that is, as a continuously unfolding series of "educative acts" as he calls them to distinguish them from what just goes on in a school—then life itself, both in and out of the classroom, is in this sense the grandest of all pedagogical exercises. Teacher, Student, and Curriculum make up the trinity of teaching and learning that are life itself.

The Danish philosopher Soren Kierkegaard certainly felt that this was the deepest meaning of "curriculum"—which he traces back to its root in Latin *currere* or "a course to run." As the etymologically-related *currents* run down the stream, so we navigate the curriculum of mortality in the cascades of our existence. Mused Kierkegaard,

> What then is education? I had thought it was the curriculum the individual ran through in order to catch up with himself. And anyone who does not want to go through this curriculum will be little helped by being born into the most enlightened age. (Kierkegaard 1969, p. 75)

The question Kierkegaard posits is, "What kind of course should we invite our students to engage upon?" We have created curricula that are designed to meet someone else's purpose—to serve the greater society, to mold children into adults that serve the system and society as defined by others, especially those persons and groups in control (Cremin 1964; Spring 2006). According to Kierkegaard, curriculum should invite the student to catch up with herself, not force her to run circles outlined by others. A good education tends to our deepest longings, enriches them, encourages the questions from which grow the tentative answers that, in turn, create fresh questions about what really matters. It is an upward spiral, this educational process, if we go about it rightly in this life.

This is a point I will wish to highlight throughout the chapter in discussing issues that, at first blush, may not seem to be related to education at all. But they are! And especially is this so when one has been labeled (or perhaps more accurately put: *branded*) with the title of "gifted." It can be a cross of gold.

For 4th grade, we were going to be bused across the railroad tracks to a predominantly-black elementary school (yes, that was the case). And so, my parents decided to send me to a K-12 private school just a few miles away. Class size: 12. Brains and more brains when it came to standard academic fare. Oh, yes, and button-down shirts and ties *every* so often I was fascinated by some of the work (SRA packets), by a few of the teachers and by almost none of my peers. And so, through high school, I poured myself into academics, sports and the piano and hoped that something good would come out of all this.

To be sure, a bunch of the 52 graduates in my graduating class would attend prestigious colleges and universities. Maybe that would be the first sign of giftedness, although I still believe that a lot of those acceptances had to do with how neurotic our parents were in securing evidence of their American success. The college stickers on the back of their automobiles were usually proof enough. I saw other bumper stickers ("My child is an honor student at Lawrence High!") as a form of violence against the child. Notice of his success is slapped on a prized object, the car, suggesting that he is himself just another one of their objects. And the brash announcement of the child's academic success (with the implicit message: "My child is better than yours") evidences with painful, even embarrassing clarity, that it is not the child that is valued so much as how the child is able to bolster the parents' narcissistic need to be at the top of the social heap.

The message to the child as he reads that bumper sticker: "I am lovable because I inflate my parents' ego with my high test scores. But what will happen if my next score is not so high? Will they still love me? Will I even still exist?" How different this is from the child-centered approach to education advocated by the great Humanist psychologist Abraham Maslow—precisely what I have been talking about throughout this book and will continue to advocate for—both in theory and in my reflections on the deeper roots of my sense of calling and my classroom practices:

> If we want to be helpers, counselors, teachers, guides, or psychotherapists, what we must do is to accept the person and help him learn what kind of person he is already. What is his style, what are his aptitudes, what is the person good for, not good for, what can we build upon, what are his good raw materials, his potentialities? . . . Above all, we would care for the child, that is, enjoy him and his growth and his self-actualization. (1968, p. 693)

Still, I knew that my 1460 SAT score meant something, but back then, it only meant that I had probably beaten out the valedictorian. But my "identity" was not the issue for my father or the schools. Indeed, I am about to talk about the journey to that "identity," both in school and out, which a student—whether in the classroom or as a student of life in general—must have affirmed in him and for him if he is to learn anything in the first place of any real significance that will stick with him.

If I were to create a list of gifts that would suggest my own, I would put classical piano at the top of the list. In a community of 20,000 which was predominantly Jewish, stellar grades and high SAT's, even prestigious college acceptances, were expected. But it was all those piano recitals, all those pieces of music by Chopin, Mussorgsky, Rachmaninoff and the like that mattered to me most profoundly as a soul. For if I were "smart," I also had a heart—and one that could express feelings that would bring people to applause, even tears. In the curriculum of life, it is the heart that God finally loves us for and judges us by. In the curriculum of the schools, it is so often the heart of the teacher that the student judges the subject-matter by . . . and then, accordingly, either learns it and makes it her own or dismisses it as irrelevant.

But the story only begins there. Gifted I was, for an adolescent. But by the time I was 19, struggling hard to keep my head above water at Princeton, I began to realize that gifts were not so easily translatable into talents that would pay royally. Working hard didn't get me very far. They only forced me to look even deeper into the part of me that lay wildly underdeveloped.

At first I chalked this up to what I came to believe was a case of noticeably low self-esteem. Later I would condemn myself for lacking vision. I have even characterized it as a problem of the will. Giftedness doesn't always imply achievement. In fact, this was almost never the case for me. Renzulli's visual definition of "giftedness" as a Venn diagram where the three circles of "Above average ability, task commitment, and creativity" intersect has been very useful to me. Remember: I'm the guy who constructs new theories on fast-food restaurant napkins between gulps of a soda and on the back of programs for theater productions during intermission! At any rate, I conclude from Renzulli that a gift is only the beginning. It comes from Heaven, from the pre-Earth-life. Hard work may very well be what one can offer to define that gift, but it is in the environment of becoming a mortal, of embodying in this realm of existence, in which one finds a crucial third ingredient: C2V2— or what I see as confidence, connectedness, voice and vision.

Family life is far more important for the full development of these gifts than I had realized. For it is within the family unit that one learns fear or faith (and thus confidence); one learns individuality or tribe (connectedness); one learns a shamed silence or an appreciated volume (voice); and one finds problems in the present or possibilities in the future (vision). In brief, if ever there was an inherently educative or miseducative cast of characters in a consummately educative or miseducative setting, it would be the family of origin, as almost all therapists would certainly attest.

As a young adult, the identification of giftedness took on new dimensions. As a very successful high school teacher (defined as connecting well with adolescents), I found that I began to see myself as gifted as a teacher. It would even lead me to take on graduate school in my early 30s, although I don't believe at all in a doctoral degree being any indication that academically I might be gifted. Perseverance would be more like it. Indeed, I had dropped out of law school after only two weeks—and I'd be damned (maybe cursed with a permanent case of low self-esteem) if I were to drop out again. And so, I trudged through a few uninteresting years of my life, at least intellectually.

One religious conversion is usually hard enough. Looking back, two conversions might simply be indicative of being a glutton for punishment. Still and all, I made it from Reform Judaism to Protestant Christianity to Mormonism and still found time and strength to carry on—never, I hope, abandoning anything along the way; but rather, incorporating everything in an upward spiral dynamic. Such is the divine mechanism of evolution, as the radical Jesuit paleontologist Father Teilhard de Chardin said is the nature of things, even of the Godhead Itself in an eternal evolution (1975). And (and here's the real punch line to all of that) this upward spiral dynamic is the essence of education, the ability to wrestle with competing, even sometimes apparently contradictory explanations of something and then taking what is best from each pole, synthesizing them and then transcending them to a new and higher perspective. Jung called this *the transcendent function.*

One thing I am hoping that this extensive exercise in teacher reflectivity is doing is to illustrate, in living Martin Kokol color, how the transcendent function is key to the process of learning, key to the calling of being a teacher, and, indeed, key (perhaps *the* key) to life itself. There is simply no separating one's narrative of oneself as an *educational Being* from oneself as a *human Being.* It puts the *sapiens* in *homo sapiens*! And so, if adolescence revealed my giftedness in music, and early adulthood in teaching, what might I write of within my midadulthood? It was so open-ended and tantalizing!

It begins with courage. Giftedness must have a pinch of that. It adds on a vision of making a positive contribution to the world. Giftedness must have at least two cups of this. And I believe such a life must also bring forth wisdom—that is, the art of care and balance that one brings to every new venture. Giftedness must have at least one cup of this. Courage, vision and wisdom. Oats, water and then salt might be the recipe.

What do I see? I see two different paths to take. One would be a good road. The other a dangerous road. I guess these paths represent my personality—and everybody's for that matter, since, as Carl Jung said, we all have a light and dark side, and we must learn to harness the energy of the dark side in the service of the good. The good road would be to satisfy my mind. It would be the organization, building and opening of a charter or private high school for the gifted. That would be my contribution to kids, families and communities, so that they could discover, develop and deliver their gifts to a world that needs them—now more than ever.

But, I also see another aspect of being gifted. And that would be to do something I don't think has been done before. It would be to conduct cutting edge research on the connections between adolescents who are gifted and those who are same-sex oriented. Although there is no literature on this idea as far as I am aware, I am absolutely convinced that there is a connection although I'm not sure, politically, if anyone wants to see such a connection. This would be my contribution to gay and lesbian kids and their families—to offer them vindication for what some of us already know intuitively so that they can fulfill the measure of their *unique* creation.

Moreover, I frame the narrative of this possibility in my own mind as not primarily a political narrative—one that is not *for* one group *against* others but as all groups *for* each other—a democratic ideal which, if it is to take hold in society at large, must play out well in the schools. Indeed, if anything is to be really relevant to the teacher and student in the core of their being, it must be taken to the sponsoring neighborhoods in which the school is situated, tried out there, added upon there, refined there, and finally encoded there as another of the multiple possibilities of democracy in schooling as well as of schooling in a democracy. Again, I cast my lot with John Dewey in his insistence that schools flourish best in a democracy and that a democracy can flourish best only when its schools are lively and lovely, galvanized and galvanizing, talented and tolerant. What I am pleading for is a pedagogy of passion.

Looking back at what was called my "giftedness," I see that, whatever else it was or wasn't, it was not really a set of gifts all laid out before me. Rather, it was an evolution—one unfolded and then utilized for a variety of purposes. Which then begets a second gift: that is to be accepted and then utilized. And finally, a third gift, which is to be understood and soon to be sought after with full intention. I have come to believe that there are no accidents. And so, I write that I may examine self, so that I might make good on the next invitation to serve, and might also be of service to the reader in her own sense of mission in her calling—a sense of mission which, however harrowed by public misunderstanding and political machinations, is (as the called teacher knows as she knows herself—indeed, only knows herself *by* knowing this) sacred. That is the third gift, the great gift: to see oneself in light of the transcendent.

It is a revolt, even a rage, against the banal in education that has, in a sense, fired my commitment to education and that defines my more fiery purposes in writing this book.

G-SQUARED: LGB

And now almost eight years have passed since writing that introduction to this chapter. I am divorced from Jon, engaged in my seventh year as a high school teacher in a small town nestled up against the Tetons, now simply an adjunct professor so that I might teach Dual Credit U.S History, and feeling a lot more my body's age, no matter how much I have gotten away with extending my young adulthood by a few decades. This will not just be about my relationship with him, my first serious relationship with a guy—but for once, it will be to backtrack all the way to my youth and adolescence to look for clues, patterns, insights and commentary regarding my relationship with males—the stunning absence of male mentors, of male friendships and then the inclusion of male attraction beginning at age 19. Along the way, I will weave this into my narrative of myself as a teacher; for, again, the two are inseparable. This is a narrative of sexual identity, yes. And we have read those before. What I want to offer is a dual tale—of my awakening knowledge of my identity, as a bisexual male and also as a teacher. I cannot render one without honoring the other. They are married within me. And this inner marriage of one's "essential" identity with one's pedagogical identity is a core truth for any "called" teacher. This is my *credo*. This I proclaim in this book. Thus, I'll give a few details of that marriage but only those necessary to make the more general points that I have just laid out to be adumbrated in the balance of this chapter.

My seven-year marriage to Jon was basically over after 5 years—I even told him in the Fall of 2016 in an e-mail, that it had come time for a divorce although we both decided to continue with a friendship. My spiritual life, expressed within a formal religious construct, had collapsed as I watched him reject organized Christianity, whereas I was certain that this was the answer for my life's journey—its goal. It offered forgiveness of my moral lapses, it offered male friendship, and, moreover, it offered Jesus as a big brother whom I could be in awe of—these would be the guiding pillars that found my life warmly entrenched with a firm testimony of the love and redemption of the Savior—certainly the Savior of my people (he was arguably the Jewish Messiah after all!) and of all people. I was looking in the Savior for that kind of acceptance, guidance, and overall identity-confirmation that Maslow, in a passage cited above, says characterizes the best teachers in how he sees and deals individually with each unique student, causing each

student to idiosyncratically blossom under the teacher's tender gaze and saga-
cious touch. And what was Christ if not the Rabbi of Rabbis—the "Teacher"
("Rabbi translated into English is "teacher") of Teachers. Even in the most
difficult highways and byways of my spiritual journey (indeed, *especially*
there), there was teacher at the heart of it all, and salvation was the curriculum
he bade me attend to in all the studious energy of my increasingly teachable
soul. My spiritual awakening and commitment, then, was of a piece, and at
peace, with my pedagogical standards and style as a wise older brother to my
class—one who had boundaries that they could not violate, to be sure, but
was also accessible to them in a way few teachers dare to be. This is not without its physical and emotional costs, but it abounds in psychospiritual graces.

But, to understand why I married Jon after just four weeks of dating (yes,
that's mania, to be sure, mixed with a large dose of anxiety disorder to complete the clinical diagnosis, but also, from a very human perspective, it was
also quite simply and understandably the need to find someone to share a life
with towards the finish line of this last third of my mortal existence), indeed
why I even chose to marry a dude, coming out of a rather solid period of LDS
church activity and testimony in New York City, I have to go back and seek
out what happened along the way to arrive at May 25, 2011. That was when I
began nightly phone conversations with him, someone I had just met online.
I'll go back to the origins of this powerful and poignant period in my life that
was ushered in with so much hope and ended in a quagmire of the first order.

In the beginning, I was raised up to be a very sweet boy, full of kindness, a
decency that was radically different from the Bruce-Springsteen-New Jersey
or even the Billy-Joel-Nassau County world in which my adolescence was
immersed. Indeed, my growth was firmly connected to what I was not. For,
I would resist being programmed to live the life of what that towering child
psychiatric theorist and practitioner D.W. Winnicott called simply but with
memorable accuracy "the false self" (1992). That is, I was hell bent on *not*
allowing my surroundings to define me, my status-obsessed, Long Island
Italian-Jewish culture to determine my destiny. New York City was a place
not to get ensnared by.

And it is true that my exposure to the world of men consisted only of two
or three NY Rangers hockey games each year, easily accessible by the Long
Island Railroad and a few escalators up into Madison Square Garden. My dad
and I would share most of these, as we would take the train into the city. Our
relationship was formal, stilted, as I would always afraid of doing something
that would get him riled up. After all, he did scare me one evening back
when I was in 8th grade, when I told some of his important friends over for
cocktails, that, indeed, I had smoked reefer just once, adding that I would, of
course, never do it again! My father came up to my room late that evening
and told me, in no uncertain terms, that he could prevent me from going to

any college. He was furious and most probably embarrassed; I was intimidated. And so, I spent the next few years trying to figure out my adolescence all by myself, upstairs, in a newly-built quiet bedroom.

And how did his anger take on shape? Why . . . in educational terms, of course! I saw that spreading my wings could cost me my future by him determining which college, if any, I could attend. This was a grim, Dickensian "Mr. Gradgrind" lesson that would replay many, many times throughout my life, as I continued to take a stand for what I believed, even though it involved putting up with criticism or threats from my father, or symbolic stand-ins for him. It was here that, despite my resistance, I was finally defeated. Finally, I came to the soul-deflating, soul-erasing conclusion never to fight again. Always looking to make others happy, even if I had to deny myself in how I would craft my own path.

Naturally, this all played out in educational terms. Turning again to Mayes (2009) in *Inside Education: Depth Psychology in Teaching and Learning,* we find a summary and assessment of the most important psychoanalytic theory regarding education over the last century. It addresses many of the issues that beset me throughout my life. In 2009, it was the first, and is arguably still the best, such exhaustive literature review on what psychoanalytic theory tells us about educational processes. In a section that I find particularly germane to the situation I have been describing in my own life and that I know very well as veteran teacher plays out in the lives of many students, Mayes clarifies what was now going on in my life, and thus I think it is worthwhile to cite him at some length at this crucial juncture where my personal biography and educational biography intersect and inflect in a fitful, fateful way. It has to do with the syndrome that Mayes calls "the model neurotic student." It was outwardly bright and shining but inwardly storm-tossed Marty Kokol to a fare-thee-well:

Certain teachers may find it difficult to see scholastic excellence as a problem. . . . Especially recently but throughout its history, psychoanalytic pedagogy has warned that prizing only academic excellence in a child not only reinforces existing neuroses in children but can actually create them. . . . Speaking of what she called a healthy "instinct for knowledge," the greatest of all child psychiatrists, Melanie Klein, proclaimed that the fundamental educational question from a psychoanalytic point of view is how to promote "a relatively undisturbed development" of that instinct, which will ideally "turn freely in a number of different directions, yet without having that character of compulsion which is typical of an obsessional neurosis" (1975 [1932], p. 103). About 20 years later, Redl and Wattenberg (1951) cautioned that a certain kind of compulsive conformism, which slavishly submits to every teacher and school rule, is not evidence of a child's adaptation to the culture of the school but is, instead, a red flag signaling that the child's behavior, at school and at home, is probably the result of fear.

Hence, "when a boy or girl shows signs of being unusually anxious to please, we should realize we have a delicate problem on our hands, instead of feeling flattered" (p. 204). For, this child, seeing himself as an object, learns only in order to confirm his servitude, not to gain intellectual and moral freedom. This confounds the whole purpose of the educational enterprise. "In a sense, each bit of good work [such students] do is a gift, or more accurately a bribe. Their actions carry this meaning, 'See, I've done what you wanted; I've proved that your wish is my command. Now, reward me by taking me under your wing. Lift me to joy by saying you like me.'" (Redl and Watternberg 1951, 203). Such pronouncements clearly echo Kohut's (1978) idea that over-intellectualization (and perfectionism in general) is often symptomatic of a narcissistic personality disorder. It also relies upon the idea of what Winnicott (1988) calls "the false self. " Fairbairn's (1992 [1940]) work is particularly insistent and poignant in calling attention to the fact that "overvaluation of mental contents" is ultimately a desperate attempt "to heap up values in the inner world" to the exclusion of external reality, and therefore is symptomatic of an unhealthy "libidinizing" of thoughts and theories, typically concluding in some form of "fanaticism" (Fairbairn 1940/1992, 15–20). And what is true for students in the schools is even truer for scholars in the university, where "'intensive inquiry' may in fact be pathological, and may lead us to consider carefully the degree of psychopathology incorporated in all research or intellectual work." (Mayes 2009, 84–5).

How much of my stellar academic performance was less (oh, much less!) about the knowledge itself and more about getting love? When this is the case, then "knowledge itself may be a defense against learning." This from the Canadian scholar Deborah Britzman, the leading figure in the field of classical psychoanalysis and education (1999, 10).

Yielding too much to others' wishes, giving up my own convictions—well, I've already shown the effect of my father's "freezing me out" and I then trying to be "the good boy," especially in school, so that that iceberg might melt just a little and a bit of fatherly warmth come through cracks to warm me up just a degree. Indeed, each new prestigious academic degree raised the affectional temperature, it seemed to me.

Being a talented performing academic monkey in school and thereby becoming an object: Was that not the root of my depression and anxiety? To lose oneself—I did it largely through the means of schooling—learning for love instead of the love of learning—this came more and more to dominate my psyche (Ekstein and Motto 1969). It stunts psychospiritual growth. Ironically, it stunts intellectual growth, since one is not likely to pursue with any great exuberance—or with any exuberance at all—knowledge that one does not value for its own sake.

Thus, a straight-A report card could be a sign of psychopathology in a student, not so much cognitive prowess, although it can be that, too, but even then, we must ask ourselves why little Juan or Stefanie has done so well if we see the tell-tale signs I was exhibiting in a student. What a difference it would have made then—a difference reverberating throughout a person's entire life, existential narrative and school narrative being inextricably bound—if I had had a teacher who saw me not as a brilliant *object* but as a gifted one, yes, but also a frightened and needy *subject*. The teacher who can accomplish that is much more like to emerge through precisely the kind of reflectivity I am not only advocating for but attempting to illustrate in this present account that you are reading about one man's life morphing from broken shards to luminous crystal. Such a teacher would have changed my life! Dear reader, *be* that teacher and make your student's heart dance, not shut down into a sort of martial-arts posture against the world.

And while on the educational and existential topic of being the best and the brightest in order to eke out a few morsels of love tossed to me, how much of my religious conversion might have been a sort of "fanaticism" mentioned above in order, again, to gain love indirectly since it was coming to me nowhere directly or cleanly in my youth but, rather, with strings attached. How much of it might have been a sublimated craving for my biological father's emotional touch and affirmation? Not to be found in Madison Square Garden. Alas, there was nothing else. I was isolated. This extended into my college years. Indeed, there was one party to attend up in the city—that of a classmate who had been raised in the Upper East Side—but I was totally out of my element. I was isolated. I was alienated. At home. At school. The two merged into a general feeling of being stranded on the airless moon. The narrative of one's life in general and one's life as student are no more separable than a creature's heart from its entire body—and the animal goes on living.

Hopefully, this little foray into deep psychological processes that affect the conscious mind and the decisions it makes, is further alerting the reader to similar dynamics in herself and her students—alerting her and altering her. Such a teacher is not a therapist, nor should she act like one. That is inappropriate and just plain unwise. However, it is not only appropriate, it is marvelous if a teacher can know enough about her own and her students' psychodynamics surrounding the processes of education that she can be a "therapeutic teacher." That is the ideal! That is what I am about in this book. That is what any teacher who wishes to enrich her student in all aspects of that student's life must aim at to achieve her noble call and fulfill her complex mission.

Why have I brought up New York so often? Simply this: as far as I was concerned, it was the epicenter of amorality, immorality, sarcasm and selfishness. Having been raised to be nice, born with substantial sensitivity, and longing to feel deeply, this was *not* the right place for such a young man to find his way. Sharon, a black American classmate, was the only woman I could really relate to—on the cheerleading squad, with a brightness in her countenance that spoke of her Christian faith, I gravitated to her in our tiny private school. But alas, I did not go so far as to ask her out. As our racial differences could even make us visual targets in our suburban community—after all, this was 1972.

Of course, there was my prom date, where I would dutifully carouse, even playing around a bit, but it was simply a time to explore. And then a year later, there was a summer romance, the one that introduced me to adulthood, with repercussions that would jolt my confidence for years. Sexual connections were easy at that age; and so, with females, things did happen. But it was a sudden eruption of male connection that fall of sophomore year in college that triggered the landslide into a psychological confusion so deep that I, to this day, cannot believe I actually finished my undergraduate studies in just four years.

Actually, there were hints of my homosexuality before I was 19—British schoolboy antics at 12 that I simply thought were fully excusable. A fascination with a young teacher (only from a distance) when I was 16. A feeling of closeness with a chaperone at 16 on the final summer camp trip—so much so that I could fall asleep on his shoulder while we drove for hours under the star-filled sky. And of course, there was that one incident Freshman year of college where, having had a few too many, I longed to connect with a classmate, only to stipulate that he was a substitute for my high school prom date—and so, nothing here!

Once the glass was broken, once there was the experience (someone enticed me from the study room of the Princeton public library), I would never be the same. He was 26. He invited me back to his place. I was ready to explode. I didn't exactly know what to do, except to avoid him from then on . . . and never study in the public library again. For after that, it became harder to seek out females to date. There were dates, there were even relationships of sorts, but the further along I travelled from 19 to 24, the more difficult it was to find significant connection that could be shared equally. Emotionally, I became stuck right there at 19. My dates began to notice. Arrested development now became not just an abstract term from a developmental psych class for me. It became a force field, an all-encompassing stasis, an insuperable weight, something like a parsec of space that turns into amber and the U.S.S. Enterprise can't break out of it despite Kirk's cool cleverness and Scotty's high-pitched expertise. I was getting well and truly stuck. Where was the teacher who could school me out of this inertia? I despaired.

In that parallel fashion, I found, as you might already have guessed, that college also was getting overwhelming for me—especially those first two years. Things would get better when I gave my life to Jesus, just after my 21st birthday. My self-confidence increased noticeably. My grades shot up to almost all As. My self-assessment would have revealed a wholeness to my being. I was grounded for the first time in years. But my sexuality was far from being "straightened" out.

And so, law school, to which I turned at age 22, doubtless to please my father, was a complete disaster. A horrific apartment mate, the shock of the NY/Miami crowd that I had been completely sheltered from being at WASPY Princeton. Dropping out after 2 weeks, I returned to NY/Princeton, hoping to connect with anyone. One girl at Princeton, but it went nowhere. Curtis at Princeton, and it happened only twice.

Ten months later, I would be moving to Claremont, California, to find my way via an M.A. into a career in Education, seeing if the Big Orange would do better for me than the Big Apple. My housemate was slightly crazy. And then, there was my first crush, up in the Bay Area, whom I had met recently. What I am trying to say is that the genuine connections were now *beginning*, just the sparks that flew, to be sure, the first-level attempts at meaning-making through intense connections. And it is interesting to me how, in retrospect, these relational connections that were starting to take only after leaving law school, which was certainly my false self, trying to please my father; but then again, the false self often constellates around an academic achievement or newly conferred title, so potent is the role of the pedagogical in the existential definition of oneself; or I followed my better angels, moved on to graduate school in education, where my heart was, where my true self could begin to break through the miasma, and where these early forms of connection began to take shape. I find not only in my own life but in my friends' lives as they feel called to teach, and I find in my students' experiences too, that the existential narrative and educational narrative either clarify each other when each narrative emanates from the true self, but horribly muddy and maim each other when either of the narratives is false. Existential narrative and educational narrative: Either we learn to wed them in fruitful union or they will split us into warring factions in an inner narratival divorce. Still, I had many miles to travel before I found myself at home educationally, spiritually, and sexually.

Within two weeks of my first semester, at the Christian fellowship, I met a wonderful young woman. We dated, but she one day told me that I seemed rather inexperienced dating women. Of course, she was right. At the same time, the man whom I rented a room from hit on me, which turned my housing situation into a seminightmare—especially since I think he was working in city government. One night, the house was broken into and there were things stolen. My innocence was now fractured. It had become too much.

At a NorCal friend's pleading, I started to attend The Open Door Community Church of Greater Los Angeles, about a 40 mile drive west of Claremont at 2244 Westwood Blvd, right off the 405. It was to become the

defining experience of my decade regarding the tension between spirituality and sexuality. If I were to simply concentrate on the former, there would
be a life for me in heaven. And of course, it was perfect timing for me to
"step up to the plate" and go for something far beyond "milk and cookies"
Christianity as the Reverend called the rest of the Protestant world. After all, I
wanted to be a man now, not a boy. Under the direction of a "Love in Action"
program, apparently written and created by the late Dr. Joseph Nicolosi, we
were invited to confess our sins, one to another (*James* 5:16), and then begin
the journey towards casting out these ungodly thoughts, for that is how I saw
these thoughts, and judged their action. Indeed, I recently read Nicolosi's
obituary in the NY Times. It was, of course, quite negative.

Dr. Nicolosi was the author or co-author of several books, including *Healing Homosexuality* (1993) and *A Parent's Guide to Preventing
Homosexuality* (2002). In a society that was becoming increasingly receptive
to gay, lesbian, bisexual and transgender people, the books were upsetting to
many people. I mention him with some trepidation for that reason. And let
me make it clear that I fully affirm that I was largely born with my sexuality
already encoded, not needing, as Nicolosi argued, to be "therapized" out of
me because it was "bad."

Nevertheless, despite Nicolosi's outrageousness in many respects, he did
make a point that stuck with me then and resonated for many years after. In
The Parents' Guide he wrote declaratively that men and women were driven
by a strong need for romantic love, but that "in homosexuals the drive is an
attempt to fulfill a deficit in wholeness of the original gender."

This idea appealed to me at the time because one of the core qualities of
my desired connection to males had been exactly this: "an attempt to fulfill
a deficit in wholeness" regarding my maleness. And so, to conclude that
summer of 1980, as a 24-year-old, I know without a doubt was a battle zone.
Not so much because I hadn't played football. Not so much because I hadn't
learned how to "get tough." Not so much because I feared my ability to get
a girl pregnant. It was much deeper than that. It had to do with the inability,
even the impossibility of expressing a viable ego-structure in my family of
origin. For that is what had been "cut off"—as I still remember the "Aha!"
wink that a therapist gave me when I told him just that!

Making father happy was the driving force of my mother and myself.
Father seemed restless beyond measure. As a child, I was to practice the piano
while Mother was preparing dinner, just in time for Father to arrive home
and expect a perfect meal on the table at exactly 7:00pm. Checking each
child to make sure that hands were washed carefully, Mother and Father then
had us sit down and give the obligatory accounts about how the day went
at school. Grades were first and foremost. Funny stories were sometimes

allowed. Mostly, it was about achievement. And, of course, there could never be enough of that.

Thus, my masculinity was never allowed to fully develop, for I as a man was simply to be judged as an extension of my Father's needs. My success was to be seen as a reflection of his, rather than proof of my own. Naturally, this all played out in educational terms. As my therapist friends assure me, you cannot start getting deeply into virtually any psychodynamic issue without education being either the cause of it or that which was most affected by it in the individual's life.

An area of depth psychological research in education that needs to be explored is parental narcissism in children's academic performance. My hunch is that many—I daresay, most—parents who demand high grades from their children and will give them "love" only when children perform well in school are, as is said in the psychoanalytic literature, "narcissistically wounded." This means that they were never healthily and heartily affirmed themselves as children. So now they symbolically try to get that love through the indirect and (let us face it) cruel means of getting it through their children's academic success. Cruel, it is also understandable. After all, all they knew of love as children was what their scholastic labors could buy them from their parents or what their academic lackluster or academic failure could get in plenty, but in falsity was well. That is the model such children may well then use in their own childrearing practices as parents and something that we need to evidence as teachers. I have no doubt that my father loved me, was a good man, and did his best for me by his lights. I honor him and in prayers, thank him daily for his financial support when needed. To see these issues clearly, and to see the effect they had on me as a student and teacher, I must aim for clarity above all else.

The reader will recall that marvelous statement by Abraham Maslow that rearing healthy children requires that parents "*care* for the child." What does that mean? It means that the parents "*enjoy* him and his growth and his self-actualization." As the Jungian analyst and theoretician James Hillman has put it, the child is an acorn. If he is to develop in health, he develops along the lines that fully express who he *is,* in and of himself, not as what he is obliged to *become* for parents. The child is loved as a *subject,* not cow-towed into being who he is *not,* in order to get pseudolove as an object. That is a lie. It is pathological. It divides the child against himself. It breeds neurosis. And, naturally, it manifests itself typically regarding educational issues.

Martin Buber would even say it is sinful to treat a child like that, as the essence of immorality, as turning the child into an abject object. My academic triumphs and terrors, my stellar performances and the agonies that underlay them—this educational narrative was interwoven with a dreadful finality into my life narrative. Even that specific and supremely sensitive part of that life narrative, my very sexuality, was inseparable from my life as a talented but tormented student. In fact, I would say that it is *especially* that part that had been at such enormous risk.

So here was the set up in my home and in the home of, no doubt, a considerable number of our students. Father and/or Mother, never having been affirmed because they either didn't perform well in school and thus were never shown real love, or did perform well but were affirmed *only* for that reason and received inauthentic love, now perpetuate that syndrome by continuing to have their own famished egos supported by more school success—this time in the form of their child's academic success.

To make matters worse, I was first born. That, of course, doubled the trouble. So different from how I would deal with my gaping hole, hoping, praying for my father (or some symbolic stand-in for him) to tell me I was alright. By definition, there was not one female who could do that. And with no male mentors to be seen anywhere in the first 32 years of my life, and with no males to be found whom I could trust, connections with males were hugely important—for the purpose *not* of instruction or even of coaching. My need was emotional, and of course the fast track for the emotional, the heroin shot that feeds right to the core is the sexual.

My sense of precariousness in the world of men, the sketchiness of who and what to be with which type of man, and when, and when it was right to push beyond simple camaraderie to more complex intimacies—this was the gender-role maze I walked down every day, and the labyrinth in which I did it was almost invariably an educational institution.

Thus, I went about trying to seek out different groups of men, to learn the fine art of discrimination. One such foray was at one of Princeton's eating clubs. It was a disaster—trying to be cocky like them didn't work; trying to excel in sports like them hadn't worked. Looking back into my formative age, because I attended a university where peer relationships were almost always threatening due to their nonstop competitive nature, my foundation was simply not in place. Confidence in most anything was sketchy at best—and this simply added to the problem of low self-confidence—which would, years later, translate into low self-esteem—yes, I've been an educator for 35+ years, but look at where it got me? In other words, the Ivy League insistence that one can measure success with money, power or fame did not serve me in my passion for teaching and mentoring. In fact, it would trigger another outbreak of "male deficit of wholeness" when I wound up living in New York at age 51—looking around at my peers many of whom had become multimillionaires while I slogged through each and every month, making it just by the skin of my teeth.

But that jumps ahead of where I am tracking. Now, emotionally scarred with the Pray the Gay Away summer of 1980, emotionally afraid of a crush that had developed but knowing so much that we could have really loved and learned from each other, had we been able to start a relationship outside of that crazy church, I returned to New York—the first time. There I finished my master's thesis on the continued need for a liberal arts education (in the wake of rising technology, now just one year from the introduction of the PC).

For the most part, intimacy with anyone was now basically shut down. I would focus on securing my next steps career-wise. Editing and then teaching became my primary focus. Dating relationships were all but impossible. To be sure, earning the trust of 16-year-olds as their young teacher was more than satisfying—it gave my life meaning and purpose. And it offered a satisfaction that was preeminent. If I couldn't help myself as an adolescent, I sure wanted to try to help a few hundred others. In depth psychology, they often talk about the therapist who can heal because, although suffering from the patient's malady (or better: precisely because of that), he has more insight into it. Such a therapist is called "the wounded healer," and he can be enormously successful if, through deep self-reflectivity, he does not project his issues onto the patient but deploys them as a tool to enhance his effectiveness in clarity and compassion. He is called "the wounded healer." May I second Mayes' notion that there can also be a salutary "wounded teacher"? (2009). And so, for five years, I was that. I did just that. And truth be told, since we are all wounded, I continue to do it. It helped and helps my students heal in an educational setting around educational issues. I was that "therapeutic teacher," I wrote about above. I was, and to some degree I remain, "the wounded teacher." And of course, Christ being the great example in the Western mythos of "the wounded healer" and "the wounded teacher," my existential narrative, pedagogical narrative, and spiritual narrative came to a powerful intersection in this zone, from which I could turn suffering into great moral advantage for my students and also for myself.

What is the mark of a "called" teacher? We have circled around that question and approached it from various points in our circumambulation. Like most things of great human import, there are various angles from which to view it—as is also the case with Picasso's "Cubist" work. One sees the subject of the painting from multiple perspectives simultaneously.

And let this be another angle to view teaching from. It's simple. Ask yourself this question: When life gets rather hairy, how do you feel about your work as teacher? Is it bothersome? Would we rather put a hold on it until life's more pressing matters get all sorted out? If so, then you are probably not meant to be a teacher. You may be a good teacher and want to continue. This is wonderful. But you are not a called teacher. However, if standing in front of a class gives you energy, replenishes you, offers hope—if teaching is leaping light in an otherwise "darkness visible," as Milton called hell in

Paradise Lost, if teaching is that light that cuts through your deepest darkness with its luminescent sword, then, my friend, you are called to be a teacher.

Five years later, after five glorious years as high school teacher/coach in suburban Miami, now up and over 30, the year at Harvard Graduate School of Education (studying to become an Administrator) became another critical year. Would I finally move up into the next step in my career? How would I handle the rather extreme loneliness that 1000 pages of reading a week would impose upon me? The novelty of being in Cambridge, Massachusetts was certainly one way to steer clear of relationships—indeed, they were too dangerous emotionally, in a year that offered zero time for any emotional risks to be taken.

On Wednesday, February 17, 1988, I decided to head to the Harvard library—a simple 10-minute walk right across Longfellow Park in Cambridge and onto the HGSE buildings. There was no internship that day—it was midwinter break—and I did not have to drive out to Lexington to shadow a principal for my school leadership class. It turned out to be transfer day for the missionaries from the Church of Jesus Christ of Latter-day Saints.

There must have been 60 to 80 suitcases all around the chapel steps. It was the first nice day of late winter—almost 40 degrees and sunny. I stopped two missionaries, made small talk and, after giving them my phone number, was swept into a really delightful next 32 days, listening to all 6 discussions that used to be requisite for baptism, committing to baptism and being loved every time I visited the mission office, just a few minutes from both my apartment and my classes. That turned out to be the key to my gaining the confidence I so badly needed.

In fact, it was so helpful, that first year of being the golden convert (Jewish background, Harvard grad student, nice guy, etc.), that my confidence soared. I was ready for much more than simply being a member of a local congregation. And so, two years later, after doctoral courses were completed at Boston U, and now ready to pack up to move to Salt Lake, I attended BYU's Summer Term at their new Jerusalem Center. There, I connected to my roots, something I had never done before—not even at my own Bar Mitzvah.

Life was wonderful. My confidence was at an all-time high. I made the move at the end of the summer of 1990, not realizing how many people were helping me make this huge transition to a new life. Dating confidently, not a gay man in sight, it was easy and arguably one of the best chapters of my life. Kris and I were "sealed"—the most solemn of Mormon ceremonies, performed only in a temple, and meant to join a couple together as an eternally creative relationship, and even *procreative*. Yes, Mormons believe in postmortal sexuality and eternal fecundity. The ceremony was performed by Elder Russell M. Nelson (who had taken an interest in Jewish converts, I was told) in the Salt Lake Temple, at the very Square I had visited 16 years earlier, where I had noticed a Star of David in their Assembly Hall. He even took the time to come and say hello to my nonmember parents (and their friends) in the waiting area of that temple who had flown in from NYC for this event. To my mother, who asked him if he had "tied the knot good and tight?," he replied "Sister Kokol" (an interesting way to address her as she was not a member!), "I am a surgeon by trade—and I tie my knots *very* tight!" The best one liner ever.

The kids were born, Arianna in 1993, always fascinated by the world around her, Natalie in the last days of 1994, beaming with a quiet and powerful confidence, and then Katie in 1997, fun-filled, full of energy. The doctoral dissertation was finally completed after several false starts, the position as Assistant Professor in the Department of Secondary Education at BYU was secured. Those were arguably the best seven years of my life. We had been able to afford a rental in Murray. But, it had come time to move down close to the university. So, what happened? Moving down to Utah County, Utah (not to be confused with Salt Lake City) was the roughest transition I think I have ever made. If life in Provo was strange enough, if the culture of BYU's School of Education was challenging enough, it was soon after buying a house in American Fork for the purpose of raising a great family that I began to feel same-sex desire all over again. Why? One possibility, looking back, is that I had forgotten to keep any previously existing male friendships. And here, I felt completely alone in a culture that I had no idea existed. Orthodoxy. Maybe similar to the Orthodox Jewish world of Brooklyn that my father had run away from—after all, how do I explain why he chose University of Wyoming after graduating from Erasmus Hall High School?

How often are major life-decisions made accompanied by a change of educational venue, focus, or status? Conversely, how many school choices lead to changes in our life-circumstances? Indeed, to change our life-circumstances is often the engine that drives educational choices that we make. "Let's see. I must have been about 22 when I met Danny. Yep. Twenty-two exactly because it was the year I graduated from college." Life's highway is marked by signposts that memorialize a particular triumph or tragedy in school; a change of heart that was instantiated by a new idea we picked up in Professor Ryan's class I was in my second year of grad school then, so it must have been in 1989; someone who gave voice to a truth that cleansed one's soul, someone whom one went on to marry; or a lecture on Zen in the last class you took in college, your final elective, a class that helped you find a peace that you thought would forever elude you.

And this is just the tip of the iceberg that is made up of countless educational exchanges that, finally, comprise the substance of your unique existence—the mark you make upon life and, even more, the marks and marvels it engraves on your spiritual skin. Why do "educative acts," as Mayes calls them, to include all of those intimate transactions with others—in school and out of school—that are one's moral essence, matter? The real question is not: "Why does education matter?" Rather, it is: "Does anything matter as much in our pilgrimage?" The teacher, specially called to embody this fact, feels, and makes this felt, in a singular way. Any wonder, then, that all that I am relating of this process leading me to 41 years of age, is festooned with all the existential clothing I was donning and doffing while also becoming a teacher, professor, and educational researcher.

The teacher—the one called in the most secret recesses of his soul to become a teacher—reaps a special fruit, but he also drinks its juice in especially bitter cups. To be a teacher, to be one *from* one's soul, to be one *as* one's soul—that is what I am about in this book, and this chapter bears witness to it for all who feel the call or who have felt and followed it throughout the pedagogical life.

No longer 24, I was now 42. Call it a midlife crisis? Three children were born and now growing, Utah County Culture was harder to adapt to than any other transition I had ever tried, and I needed to be fed emotionally as my wife was starting to distance herself from me as I sensed I was simply too much of an extravert for her comfort.

I found a really good therapist in Orem and, for the next three summers, we explored. Until one day, I blurted out that I thought I might be gay. "Well that explains everything," he sagely replied.

By 2001, the marriage was in big trouble. We had not built a solid friendship, which I had not understood was a sure foundation for a long-term relationship. I remember the next two years only as a kind of ongoing nightmare. We clung on to whatever remained of the hoped for Disney-like life when, in 2004, my life got more complicated. Work was about to become a disaster.

Utah Valley State College seemed OK. BYU's program was being phased out and so the Dean wrote me a wonderful letter of recommendation to be hired over at UVSC, just a few miles away. The new assignment saw six, maybe seven courses to develop and teach, and being invited to become a faculty senator was actually very rewarding. But as I went up for tenure on March 11, 2004, there was a problem. I was not from there. And some students were a bit taken aback by my occasional comments that would be labeled as "liberal."

What happened over the next little while is but a blur. Going up for tenure, blowing past the Chair and the Dean's lack of recommendation. Hoping to be given the green light by the Faculty Committee. It was a daring political move. And then, more importantly, there was my going to the SLC Pride Parade on June 13, 2004. And that was the bombshell. A senior administrator called me in just a few weeks later. "We have a problem. . . . You were seen at an event that promotes an alternative lifestyle. A major donor is very concerned about this. And in a nutshell, I would strongly advise you to find new work. And you are not to say anything about this meeting. Because if you do . . . "

I have dwelt throughout this book on the subtle psychological and spiritual intermeshing of one's life narrative and one's educational narrative. Usually, this is a subtle wind that blows around our heads throughout our lives. But for the teacher, it can be a scalding blast of furnace air in the teacher's face in not-so-subtle, indeed quite harsh monetary and legal terms when it comes to the teacher publicly associating himself with an unpopular cause. He is, after all, a public figure. The community has its eye on him. What happens when a teacher presses a hot button issue in the way the community doesn't like? A Pride parade in the heart of Mormondom, a religion that is particularly traditionalistic and moralizingly strict, is bound to catch the community's attention and (in my case) likely to incur its wrath, often from some highly-placed people in that community.

During that very month, I had recognized that it had come time to move out of the family home. To be sure, I had gone to this parade rather than to church with the family. And so, I needed to leave. I secured a new apartment in Draper, north of Provo, just up into Salt Lake County (more progressive). I even had it painted different colors before move-in day. As I packed up the U-Haul, the kids were told by their mother on their way up to Park City. That outing was my idea for them to enjoy a hotel room for a night while I moved out. It was a blur. And then it was summer break.

Giving up on the church was easy. They had no answers for me. The next year was a blur until spring break of 2005, when things morphed from being a blur to a sterile, blank field. I started to "white out." In fact, I was becoming barely semicoherent in conversations. When I finally had attained a sufficient degree of orientation and knew that I needed to get to a hospital, I went at 6am. The emergency room nurse began by taking my vital signs. My blood pressure was 235/195. Stunned, she told me I could have easily died five minutes earlier. I called John, my spiritual dad and my friend from the get-go during my time in the LDS Church. Both his mother and his oldest daughter had been missionaries in Cambridge Massachusetts 16 years earlier when I had started this next chapter of my spiritual journey, which, as in Dickens' *A Tale of Two Cities,* had begun as "the best of times" but now found me shipwrecked and stranded in an emergency room—a dead man walking through "the worst of times." He asked me to trust him on this and told me to pack up an overnight bag and to come up to his home. And then, we went over to Utah Neuropsychiatric Institute, and, after a call to my folks explaining the expenses of the place, got me checked in. All I remember was how crazy the two roommates were that weekend—the first, a teenager who had bought heroin from someone in the Bountiful benches, an older suburb of Salt Lake; the second, a businessman—a businessman who used the same dealer! They both paced all night long.

I was finally released after a friend had come out to see me. I guess I was just a bit incoherent. A week later, back to work at UVSC, trying to teach classes the first day back from spring break, I guess I was still a bit incoherent, and so, an emergency meeting with an administrator, a generous offer by an older colleague to give me a bunch of his sick days, and out I went. My amazing mother had come out to Utah to be with me, and got me on a plane the next day, to head back to New York City. And within days, a lifelong friend, now a medical doctor, found a therapist with whom I started seeing. From there, it was a good five months in my folk's apartment, to begin a two-year healing, seeing a therapist, returning to Orem to report to a very senior administrator who was the only one who gave me a running chance to work, as he offered me a position for a full academic year before I had to move on. Others told me that this was an extraordinary offer and that I should take it. And so I did.

At this point in my saga, the interaction of my four narratives—MLK the teacher, MLK the spiritual seeker, MLK the bisexual man, and MLK the existential being—is so multiplex, narratival strands weaving in and out of each other in such complex designs—that it becomes impossible to say where one starts and the other stops. Thus, it is in the life of every called teacher—a fact that can emerge in special, even exquisite, pain when one is in crisis. Some years ago, the author Irving Stone wrote a bestseller entitled *The Agony and the Ecstasy* about the life of Vincent van Gogh. Too bad he used that title already. It would work as the title of so many called teachers. Truly, their name is Legion, and I am one of them.

I didn't know what to do, adrift upon this uncharted ocean. One of the more useful things I did was to attend a seminar recommended to me by a friend. It revolved around the ideas of "getting tough" and "learning how to be a man." These may seem corny precepts around which to form a weekend retreat, but it worked for me at the time—all the more so since it was my masculinity that was at stake here. How would I redefine myself in such a way that my sense of masculinity was not imperiled by inner condemning voices but was, instead, set free to explore new horizons under the liberating pull of a new vision of what it was to be a man—in my case, a bisexual man? This ancient issue in my life had come to its most extreme manifestation in the form of a near-death visit to an emergency room. Once and for all, I had to face it or else be consumed and finally obliterated by it. And should it come as any surprise that it was a psychoeducational retreat that first came to my aid—another *educative process* would help school me—a veteran teacher but also now a student of myself—as this process got underway literally as a matter of life and death?

By this, I don't mean to say that I was, or was indeed looking to be, "cured" by this retreat. For instance, a couple of us were powerfully attracted to each other—not just sexually but recognizing kindred spirits in each other.

Mankind Project's New Warrior Training Adventure in late summer 2006 was the second such activity I got involved with. This was where things started to open up. And I found myself full-on realizing that I was probably more gay than straight. And I was at peace with it. Finally. A couple of essentially educational seminars had helped me arrive at this place of acceptance, even excitement at the possibility of growth, opening up new vistas of possibility where before there were only dark clouds on a dire, shrinking horizon. I had turned 50. I headed back to New York after that weekend. It was time for me to make a new life.

Little did I know that I would return to the LDS church. One major thread at a time, I thought to myself. It turned out that the ward in Manhattan was wonderfully progressive. I moved into a quiet apartment just across the street from Julliard, where I had been accepted as a 10-year-old for their children's program. Alas, my father had forbidden it (my hunch is that he might have detected that I was gay even then and feared that going to a music school would "expose" me to a population that he felt it his duty to "protect" me from), and somehow, my mother knew all along that that was where I belonged. So, 40 years later, here was this wonderful tiny apartment where I could even hear the music from their students playing in the square floating up to my 18th story apartment.

Pretty soon thereafter, I would begin feeding the missionaries—a standard practice among devout Mormons of support both for the doctrines of the church and for the missionaries who were out wanting to teach them with an eye to gaining even more members in this rapidly growing church. The teacher in me, too, was no doubt rising to give aid and comfort to these young men who now found themselves in essentially a teaching role as missionaries. The more deeply one is committed to teaching in the classroom (those "educational processes" that Mayes writes about), the more one sees them going on outside of the classroom in the form of "educative processes." Shakespeare wrote that "all the world's a stage." To the called teacher, it might better run: "All the world's a classroom."

Four years in NYC, mostly taking care of my dad, whenever I was not teaching or supervising, which I always found not merely interesting but galvanizing, even life-giving. I also found myself investigating more closely than I had ever done before the world of my grandparents and great-grandparents to be a "balsam to my soul." These investigations of love took me to the lower

East Side, up to the Bronx, and to Coney Island Avenue in Brooklyn. My father was sliding into his last couple of years of life. Beginning with a fall, just 30 minutes after I left him at his apartment, with my mother out of town, my sister called me to say that our father had been picked up in an ambulance and was in an uptown hospital emergency room. I started to wonder if I would need someone new to protect me from the world. Today, I wonder if that was one of the triggers to finding a male in my life to replace my father, no matter how little heart he might have. For I knew that he cared about me deeply. And after so many years of misunderstanding, I was starting to be able to care about him significantly.

As the months progressed, and as I continued to fly back to Utah to see my kids, to be there for their choir concerts and their volleyball matches, my behavior remained as a "Latter Day Jesuit." For the most part. I knew I was not going to be able to date women anymore. And so, it was simply if I was going to remain single and alone in the big city for the years to come or whether I would find a man to settle down with in the last major chapter of life, for being alone is torturous, all the more so to an extrovert like me. I knew I was unhappy.

I wondered how I was going to leave, after my father passed away. My mother had her friends. And suddenly, there was the invitation to teach online for Touro College's graduate school of education. I jumped at the chance and started looking for apartments in Salt Lake. But I made the mistake of telling my kids that I was moving back. Because just two days after my oldest daughter's high school graduation, I decided to meet up with this guy whom I had been talking with for about 10 long nights. He made me a beautiful welcome fire up on the land above his mother's house. And, rather than staying calm and composed, I fell for him.

Mormon culture is big on marriage. And to be sure, marriage is crucial if one is going to be sexual. Yes, call it 1950s America. I know, I know. Of course, I was aware that this was a gay marriage and that that fact would lead to some resistance even in the very progressive Mormon community of New York. But that was not uppermost in my mind. Call it innocence. Call it such a fervent wish to be accepted that I put it in the back of my mind. But what was uppermost for me in this decision is just that I had to do it right—and declare to everyone that I was now "taken."

And so, on July 22, 2011, after just dating for 6 weeks, thinking this was my last chance at 55 to find a wonderful male (for you know, as they used to say, us gays get our senior citizen card the minute we turn 40), we married in Connecticut, where his 9th great grandfather had come to make a new life in 1640. Just over two hours' drive from New York. Where my mother would enjoy a day trip. Where my sister and her family would stop off on their way to see their daughter farther up the coast. And where my aunt would fly up from Miami to join my mother at the wedding ceremony with a total of eight in attendance. It was, looking back, a mockery of marriage. Not because it was a gay marriage! No. It was, rather, because it had been so hastily organized.

As my daughters were in NYC visiting their grandmother, I had told them just days before about all of this in a restaurant, where they shouted, slammed down the silverware, cried, and stormed out of the place. I should have known *right then and there*. The innocence and complete clarity of the three of them. But I missed the obvious cue and simply kept running into my mania. And told the moving company of a destination with a different address. Where I would teach 24-year-olds mostly online along with 16-year-olds as a substitute teacher for the local school district. And where I would begin a new chapter of life.

So, what was the attraction? That is most important to get at. It was to engage with a male in every possible realm: The spiritual, intellectual, emotional, physical. Here again, my convictions as a teacher informed my life as a man in a relationship. I made an extended case for this in a chapter I contributed to a recent book, *Developing the Whole Student: New Horizons in Holistic Education* (Mayes 2019). Using Mayes' categories, I reflected on my career as a master teacher and on the student's holistic needs from seven perspectives which cater to the student in the various domains of his and her being and acting in the world: The Organismic, the Emotional, the Empirical-Procedural, the Legal-Procedural, the Phenomenological, the Immanent, and the Ontological. These boil down in simpler language to the physical, the psychological, the mechanical, the social, the deep experiential, the spiritually-saturated natural, and the transcendent. I had hoped that the relationship with him would tick off all of those boxes. It didn't. One of the thrills of teaching (when one is not under the gun of state surveillance of standardized curriculum and instruction) is that it can make happen in the classroom what it is much harder to realize in the outside world. For the teacher who can accomplish this, his or her students will remember the class as one of the high points in his life, against which he will often measure the rest of his life in the "real" world.

This is a primary reason that one's "school narrative" is so vital and why we do well to make it as vibrant and abundant as we possibly can. For, it becomes an existential compass for the rest of one's life—a shining vision of the intellectually, ethically, and emotionally high in one's life. So, it had always been for me, and it is this excellently bright vision of the possible that I projected onto the idea of marriage with him. But the Camelot of the classroom is not often found in the too-often dreary desert of daily life. Is it any wonder that I—fundamentally the radical idealist—have never been able to leave the classroom for any great length of time?

As for my testimony of the Church, I remained confused. On occasion, I attended the local congregation. During the winter of 2014–15, I moved down to Salt Lake to help my friend Marc with his start-up company (I still had my full-time online position teaching graduate students out of Touro College). And when I chose to return to Wyoming in early April 2015, I was struck with a very painful kidney stone. Apparently, I hadn't drunk enough water for a long time. To be sure, it was a wake-up call to my sense of mortality.

Suddenly, thanks to an out-of-the-blue ad in the local paper regarding an opening, I secured an fascinating half-time position as a social studies teacher at Teton High School in Driggs, just 45 minutes west of Jackson Hole, over the Teton Pass. The Fall of 2015 would be the start of a fantastic two plus years of teaching (grading and a bit of Skyping with) graduate students who were studying to become high school teachers online *and* teaching high school students, live. Both were enriched by the other. Of course, I had to drive the Teton Pass—against traffic during the long winter. Indeed, I had occasionally seen four headlights coming at me head on during those early morning commutes, which is a bit nerve wracking on a two-lane mountain highway! And then, even more eye-opening, it was the moose. The moose which suddenly jumped over the guardrail and started to run alongside of my car. Who then decided to lower his towering rack and smash into my rear door, only to lift his rack and shred off my ski rack! $8000 damage. But, without hesitation, I continued that October morning (rut season, I was told!) right into the high school parking lot where I would be given high fives in the hallways during lunchtime by some of the seniors, saying "Welcome to the Valley, Kokol!."

What I noticed right from the beginning, teaching government to high school seniors was that some of them (those who were LDS) had a very obvious light in their countenance. It was more than confidence. It was more than kindness. And I started to realize that I was missing something, something so significant that I would have to deal with it pretty soon. There was something special about them. And I had not realized that my own light had gone into hiding to a large degree. Not that I was evil. Not that I was clueless. Just that there was this feeling that mine had dulled. And once again, the tension between spirituality and sexuality. Mine (I wonder: was the rutting moose a symbol or, as Jung would put it, a synchronicity of that tension in my life? Was the moose another "lesson" being sent me by an Invisible Teacher beyond? I sometimes think of synchronicity as lessons from the Pedagogical Universe, although the meaning of those lessons is often very hard to discern. And of course, it became clearest to me in the classroom, where the called teacher finds that he both gives and receives some of the most important lessons in his life.

The New York online position ended at the end of 2017. And thus, the fun of earning this two-pronged salary came to an end. My finances were now tumbling. And I was not going to stiff my daughters with their college expenses.

Things spiraled down in the marriage. Our orbit seemed to decay with each new day. There was nothing left for it but divorce. The divorce would not take very long. Through mediation, I chose to pay him a lump sum of money so that I might stay in my new house, with potential future memories for my daughters and their future families.

For, memory is also a great teacher. In remembering, we do not simply call clear, objective, cold "facts" to current awareness. No. We extract the meaning out of those moments by relating them to our present as lenses to view that present, which in turn creates grounds for imagining a meaningful future. To remember in this way is an intensely ethical act. It is indeed the act I am engaged in in these pages, remember (in your presence, my reader) who and what I was so as to construct something ever closer to what I, in my highest dreams, wish to become—learning how to do that in this present of "educative acts" that may lead to a future of greater wisdom in me and thus, even greater potential as a guide for my students.

In his *Remembrance of Things Past,* Marcel Proust came to understand himself with a thoroughness few of us will ever remotely even imagine because he dwelled constantly within what he called "the vast structure of memory." I picture that "vast structure" as another kind of schoolhouse, where the curriculum of time shapes us one and all into more than beings of an unreflective present but into beings who may meditate on our "time" and what happened in it in order, perhaps, one day to transcend that time. Ah, Time the Teacher!

G-SQUARED: SHAME & GUILT:
LEADING TO INDEPENDENCE

What has happened to me more recently, as I approached the wonderful age I thought about as a boy while listening to the Beatles singing "When I'm 64"? It is this: shame is powerful. It hurts when I have been blamed for being Jewish, as when I first got to college. It hurts when I have been blamed, ostracized, fired illegally and even threatened with my life for being LGBTQ. And then there is shame's cousin: guilt. Feeling so horrible because not only would a father, a religious leader, even God himself, look down upon me, but because there is no escape, unless one goes *directly* to the one who has the power to forgive, and, while he's at it, to explain.

This explanation had come to me on May 7th, 2011 in a special place to Mormons. The Sacred Grove, located in Palmyra. New York, west of Syracuse, east of Rochester. It is the place where Joseph Smith claimed to have first seen in the flesh God the Father and Jesus Christ. There, I decided to see for myself what the place looked like and maybe even what it felt like. And so, having driven six or so hours up to Western New York from the "City," with four young Mormon acquaintances, I entered the grove, headed right, past the picnic benches, "into the woods" (as my middle daughter's play she had performed in just recently was called), as the boys all went left. And after about three minutes, walking deep into those woods, I slowed down and stopped in a very peaceful place. That is when it happened.

WHAT DID I SEE?

Well, if you took high school chemistry, you know about the periodic table. And quietly, there, about 20 feet from me, in the middle of thin air, just about 3 feet above my own height, was a periodic table—about 25 feet in length, 15 feet in height. And suddenly, with all the elements in their place, Na and Cl moved out and lit up. I stood there, rubbing my eyes. But, there they were. And then a voice (yes, a quiet peaceful voice) asked me, "What is that?" And I quietly stated, "That's Sodium and Chlorine!" "Good" was the reply—and then another question: "And what kind of a bond do they make?" "An ionic bond" I whispered, remembering well from my 10th grade Chemistry class, with Mr. Wong, my teacher and tennis coach still clear in my memory. My sacred narrative in the Sacred Grove and my narrative as a student—again, at a determining moment in both of those narratives, a literal apotheosis unfolded before my eyes as all my narratives again blended—but this time into perhaps one of the grandest moments in my life. Or was it just a "moment"? Was it not rather what T.S. Eliot called "the moment in and out of time" and "the intersection of planes of existence," where "the past and future are conquered and reconciled"?

And in a gentle, even slightly humorous touch, possible only from the Divine Teacher, who as the Master Teacher of the Universe, understands and perfectly employs and evokes a smile even in the midst of the most important matters (and here, the curriculum was my life itself!), I saw the two elements on this huge periodic table receding into the chart. And just 10 seconds later, different elements started to emerge and light up—N2, then O2, then H2, then He2 followed by all the Noble gasses. They just slowly came out from the "board" and then lit up. "What are these?" was the question in my mind, my heart, my soul. "Easy! Those are Nitrogen, Oxygen, Hydrogen, Helium and all the rest of the Noble gasses!" I replied quickly.

After a moment of thunderous silence, I heard: "Yes, my son, and so what I want to remind you is that just as most of my bonds at the elemental level are ionic—that is, opposites attract—a few of my bonds at that level are covalent:

that likes make a pair!" I was happy to be given such a lesson. But the next comment has become the response of my lifetime. "So that you know, just as I do this at the elemental level, so I do also at the human level. Most of my creation follows the principle 'opposites attract,' but sometimes I create according to another of my grand principles: 'Likes make a pair.' I know you, Martin Lawrence Kokol. I made you. I love you. Do not even worry about your attraction. It is perfectly acceptable to me! Now, just remember, people may hate you, they may revile you. You may even lose your church membership. That is not a problem for me, nor will it be for you. Just remember one thing: Be first class in all your dealings with your fellow man, and all will be well. Now go and love and fear no more." God revealing Himself to me, about the source of my pain, as a high school chemistry teacher with the alchemical substance of pure love. The archetypal "Divine," a portion of it embedded, I believe, in all the acts and arts of great teaching—it manifested itself to me in a simple, quiet vision in the Sacred Grove, which now became a Sacred Classroom, with the omnipotent, everlasting God manifesting Himself in what must be His favorite form in dealing with His children: As a Teacher.

And just like that, I was given a love that was no longer conditional—that is, "I love you IF . . . ." No, here was the moment of triumph. "I love you. Period." I had come to this moment of my life—and now I was ready to turn over all the chapters on Shame (who I am) and on Guilt (what I have done) and could now proceed towards Independence.

G-SQUARED: PUTTING THE PIECES TOGETHER

When in the course of a man's life, it becomes necessary for him to journey farther, deeper, and with greater purpose, it behooves him to see that Giftedness and Gayness must have a companion. For they are meant to lean up against each other, with hopes that all will be well. Filling in the space between, there comes a power that cannot be described merely by labelling. For it appears in a place and a time that offers power, significance and glory above all.

What I propose here to conclude this chapter is that we take a look at both sides of the coin: the gifted side and the LGBTQ side. For both have been neglected to a variety of degrees in this country,

There is absolutely nothing in place to assist our gifted young people. The standard answer is that "we have Honors and AP classes to offer them." And it would seem that that should suffice! Popular culture suggests that LGBT people concentrate in cities or on the coasts. However, consider the demographics: Of the roughly 19 million LGBT people in the US, between 2.9

million and 3.8 million live in rural communities. Experiencing at least some sense of isolation is common for LGBTQ people in rural areas.

FOR THE GIFTED SIDE OF THINGS

Building from these four qualities to our lives, we can conclude that:

"Heartwork" is about *passion*, "mightwork" is about *power*, "mindwork" is about *precision,* and "spiritwork" is about *peace*. These are the four driving forces in human growth, forces that we must address.

The heart's desires are: sincerity, hope, admiration, understanding, empathy and compassion.

The mind's desires are: knowledge, respect, integrity, enlightenment, curiosity, and purpose.

The will's desires are: convictions, courage, choice, faith, humility, and obedience.

The spirit's desires are: connection, devotion, gratitude, kindness, harmony and stillness.

As students (and learners in general) grow, there is the mindful desire for *knowledge*, not just memorization, and there is the heartfelt desire for *understanding*, not just enjoyment. Then there is the will's desire for *courage* to learn new things, not just to demonstrate mastery. And finally, there is the spirit's desire for *connection*, not just to achieve stillness.

Looking at some of the great civilizations of our planet, I propose that the following ideals might be picturesquely and fancifully represented by associating each one with a country or area as it exists in the popular imagination. 1) From Europe comes *truth*; 2) from Africa: *honor*; 3) from China, *wisdom*; 4) from Japan, *beauty*; 5) from America: *liberty*; and, 6) from the Holy Land: *charity*. And then, juxtaposing the ideals to the core desires, we get: the longings of the heart, the workings of the mind (and, from both the will's securing achievement and the spirit's offering of dreams), and the stirrings of the soul.

Implications for teacher and student: if we juxtapose school achievement and adolescent dreams, we have this:

1. From the mind, the teacher motivates
2. From the heart, the teacher inspires
3. From the will, the student performs
4. From the spirit, the student aspires

Implications for K–12 curriculum development in the USA: (from the ideals to the subjects taught):

1. Truth: Mathematics and Sciences
2. Honor: Foreign Languages and Coding
3. Wisdom: American and World Literature
4. Beauty: Art, Music, Theatre, Architecture
5. Liberty: US and World History, U.S. Government, Economics
6. Charity: World Religions and other electives

What does this offer the gifted student? Liberty to explore far and wide, charity to love selflessly.

In the end, adolescence is a time to dream, not just a time to achieve. We now see how and why we must offer both. But there is one more ideal, a seventh, with its four components: From the Mind: Peace; from the heart: Compassion; from the will: Persistence; from the spirit: Joy.

Finally, school must become a place for the whole student, not just a place for the mind and body. And for the gifted student, it is not just "throwing" Honors and AP courses to them, as if throwing pieces of meat to hungry wolves. For this will not suffice. We must all learn that it's not just a mind that is a terrible thing to waste; it is the heart and soul that are a tragedy to ignore. Educational ideals—for the gifted, the talented, the average and the challenged learner—*must* be reunited with core desires, and this has eye-opening implications for both curriculum development and instructional strategies. It is now up to us to create the blueprint and supply the details. Considering both NCLB and CORE have been dismissed, it's time to start conceptualizing, drafting and implementing a structural change, so that the G/T teacher can raise the bar and that G/T students can begin a satisfying work on their way towards a fulfilling education.

In the next chapter, I get more specific about constructing a model of education that covers the lifespan. Accordingly, it is to that that I now turn.

Chapter 3

Journeys of the Heart

Shades of Darkness, Shades of Light

In trying to analyze today's educationally impoverished high school student, one senses in him and her "a straining to say something, a search for an inwardness that one knows one has, but it is still a cause without an effect. That is, the inner seems to have no relation to the outer" (Bloom 1987, 155). Naturally, our outer life involves the search for a successful physical or material life in addition to how we fit (or choose not to fit) into external socioeconomic and politico-cultural conditions and contexts. Our inner life is largely comprised of the emotional or the intellectual potential of each and every student and teacher. Cognitive psychology deals admirably with the intellectual side of the outer life. As for the student's inner life, what Irene Salzberger-Wittenberg (1989) called *the emotional experience of teaching and learning,* it is to the depth psychologies and their educational applications that we must turn (Britzman 2001, Mayes 2020).

Outer life is louder than the quiet reserved place of the inner life. It is in the balance between the outer and the inner—that is, in being able to live successfully in both the outer and the inner worlds—that we arrive at the realm of the moral; for, it is here that inward intention and outward action synthesize in the form of deeply considered, profoundly felt, and practically efficacious action in the world. Education to be ethically viable must therefore address the claims of both the outer and inner life—as it were: the introverted side of our experience along with the extroverted side of that experience.

Here it is necessary to make a distinction between two things which, although related at innumerable points, may still be differentiated. They are the spiritual and the moral. Spirituality, as I will use that fraught term, pertains to the delicate motions of the inner being in communication with the divine within, the image of God—the *imago Dei*—as it presents itself to each human being in a way that is, for whatever reasons, best suited to that individual (Heisig 1979). Ethics typically pertains to the robust action of the

65

self in the outer world of social interaction, fiscal and jurisprudential controversy and resolution, and political action; and it tends to be regulated by
more general codes of behavior that are basically incumbent on everyone to
heed. One might say that spirituality is a more introverted process; morality,
more extroverted.

Both the spiritual and the ethical are crucial in helping the student develop
into a healthy, integral individual. Religion is in this sense a balancing act
of the spiritual and ethical, a way of remaining true to the individual's inner
vision as a unique spark of the Divine flame, but also attending to the outer
systematization of virtue in codes of conduct as they are laid out in a religious
tradition's foundational narratives and sacred texts (which are often the same
thing) and then, later, formally codified as law (Bruner 1996). These codes
will vary from tradition to tradition, culture to culture, epoch to epoch—and
yet there is a core of values that tends to remain fairly constant despite this
vast geographical and historical range (Giddens 1990). Because we care
about our children as functioning in a good society but equally care about the
child seeking the divine in his or her own way, it becomes clear that a moral
education is not "sermonizing to children against their instincts and pleasures,
but rather in providing a natural continuity between what they feel and what
they can and should be" (Bloom 1987, 80). What is sought, then, is the connecting of intellect and sentiment with potential and destiny.

Back in the 1980s, which saw the meteoric rise of the Fundamentalist
Christian movement with political implications with the likes of Jerry
Falwell, as well as personal implications with a host of televangelists such
as Robert Schuller, Jim Bakker, Oral Roberts and others, what had already
taken place was the individualization of morality, a morality that had become
"personal, not social, private, not public" (Bellah 1996, 231). In a nutshell,
the discussion of morals and of moral education had been shoved into the
closet of American life.

The problem we now confront is that in a values-relative world, such
as that of postmodernism, many feel that there is no way to determine an
"ethical core" to the curriculum. Values clarification—or, helping the student discover what is fundamentally important to him personally without
attempting to assert that certain things are wrong or right in a manner that
goes well beyond his personally preference—was a "middle approach in
teaching "ethics" in that it dealt with ethical questions but did not lay down
any ethical absolutes. It was helpful in identifying issues and perhaps in pri-
oritizing preferences or even possible courses of action for students, but it
did not provide a foundation upon to plot those courses or prepare for those
actions in an objectively principled way (Lickona 1991). But, now that values
had been stripped away from the foundation of actual good and actual evil,
the only choice left was either to impose values (an authoritarian approach

which never works educationally) or to quit permissively do without them (a permissive-indulgent approach, which is a short road to chaos). Most of the time, mainstream America chose the former course for inculcating the next generation with salutary codes and thus prepare them for ethical action. This has ever been a function of a culture's educational system (Pai and Adler 2011). Now, in these very strange times in which we live, that educational *desideratum* has been problematized, satirized as "small minded," and almost entirely dismissed.

In other words, with values seen as a solely individual matter, the "introverted," particularistic side of the individual was stressed, but at the expense of objective social interaction and democratic growth. On the other hand, with values seen as a strictly social phenomenon, necessary for the smooth functioning of a nation but not necessarily resonant, rich or compelling for the individual, ethics ran the risk of becoming a matter of mere conformism. This lands us on the horns of a dilemma: on one "horn," a personal, highly idiosyncratic "spirituality" that is socially unresponsive and perhaps even socially dangerous, if not, indeed, fatal; on the other hand, a socially functional set of standards to live by in relative harmony, but also without individual growth of consciousness in existential courage; merely "going along to get along."

But, before we continue, certain terms need further clarifying.

1. *Values education* involves learning to identify one's *own* priorities and is thus best seen as an internal, individual, and (in a word) "subjective," intuitive process, not an objective, social one—one, that is, that is generally held to be true across different cultures in different physical locales and world-historical epochs (Fay 2000). Kant spoke of these intuitively accessible, universally acknowledged, and everywhere incumbent values as *categorical imperatives.* For instance, in no culture is gratuitous killing considered anything but reprehensible, and only in a few exotic and eccentric cases is brother-sister incest considered acceptable (as in the pharaonic *hierosgamos* in ancient Egypt, where brother and sister marry in accordance with a certain ancient religious process); and in no culture is parent-child sexual intimacy looked at with anything but repulsion as being craven and abusive almost beyond imagining.
2. *Successful mastery* is the foundation upon which self-esteem can be constructed.
3. As C.S. Lewis (1960) proclaimed in his educational classic *The Abolition of Man, character education* involves the development of good traits; these are usually considered important to one's peers or social group. Successful mastery begets honor and respect.

4. *Moral education* involves learning to recognize and to choose right from wrong; this is usually considered important to one's God. Successful mastery begets virtue and power.

How, then does one study the topic in educational theory of how to contribute in the classroom to the formation of a moral person? This has, of course, been a prime topic in educational theorizing from Plato (1960) in *The Republic* to Whitehead (1964) in *The Aims of Education* and Adler (1982) in *The Paideia Proposal,* and up to this present moment. From the outset, it would be most helpful to place moral education alongside the other educations that students receive as part of a formal and informal curriculum. We all grew up with the term "PE" or physical education. And, of course, there is also the cognitive education that schools are primarily concerned with. Educators also speak of a social education, or at least the socializing process that is so important for all youngsters and, which it is argued, public schools (as opposed to homeschooling or online learning) can best offer. Primary educators are also very aware of an emotional education that goes on in the classroom, a security that is surely important for future professional as well as personal success.

That we tend to think of emotional education as a focus only for the earlier years of schooling, becoming less and less important as students move up the ladder towards graduation, is tragic—an undeniable indication of how little the psychological and spiritual side of the student is valued as he or she matures, even erased. This turns education in the higher grades into a merely functional mechanism, what the Libertarian educational theorist Joel Spring has called a "sorting machine" that does not so much educate the individual "worker-citizen" but, rather prepares her for what kind of cog she will be in the vast corporate economy/surveillance state that our society increasingly devolves into. In a more holistic environment, the child finds within herself many inner potentials, not just "marketable" ones, and is treated as an integral and empowered being-in-the making, not as a disempowered "unit" whose primary importance lies only in his social utility, just the kind of antieducation and psychospiritual paucity that some educational theorists manage not only to tolerate but to advance.

Such theorists—Moe and Chubb (2009) come to mind as prime exemplars—view the child in quintessentially unethical terms as "human capital"— a phrase that must make any spiritually-called teacher shiver to his very soul. And so, moral education is to be seen not only as key in its own right but as a political resistance to forces that would objectify the student. Education that does not objectify the student but honors his or her legitimate "subjectivity"

Table 3.1. The four quadrants of a complete education: Impediments and accomplishments

Domain	Problem	Desire	Cure
Intellectual	Boredom	Career	Finding motivation
Emotional	Loneliness	Friendship	Finding rich connections
Physical	Lethargy	Strength	Developing strength
Spiritual	Emptiness	Core Truth	Developing a sense of mystery

must, therefore, contain moral education as one facet of a total education that *must* be available for any student.

In advocating for holistic education, one may start by imagining what the result of an impoverished education in each of holistic education's domains would look like.

In the world of physical education, we might find a lack of sturdiness, strength, or coordination. Muscle development as well as hand-eye abilities would be left incomplete. We might say that the body had gone "flabby." In the area of cognitive education, we would be heartbroken to find illiteracy. Mental skills with both numbers and words would remain underdeveloped. Educators would say that the mind lacked sharpness or keenness. In the area of social/emotional education, we would be greatly concerned with the reclusive or the withdrawn child and, indeed, with all of the children, who had been taught merely to succeed at all costs. The ability to interact well with one's peers would be missing. We might say that the boy or girl, even the emerging young adult lacked friendliness, geniality, or graciousness. A poor social/emotional education would leave a youngster cold, detached, or reserved. One might comment that a sensitivity was lacking.

And what of a poor moral education, which is our primary area of interest at this moment? The student would not so readily or deeply gain attributes such as being noble, principled or virtuous. Moral competence that might have developed goodness, conscientiousness, scrupulousness, honesty, decency, and modesty would not, by my reckoning as a master teacher, mentor, and eventually a friend to my students, be nearly so evident in my students' lives without moral education as with it. We might find highly competent specialists here in this field or that, but this group could hardly be characterized as vibrantly *ensouled* but rather as desouled with what is called in clinical psychology "flat-affect"—referring to the apparent lack of emotion about almost everything. In this mode, the world is "for them what it presents itself to the senses to be—unadorned by imagination and devoid of ideas" (Bloom 1987, 134). Flat affect accompanying an inner desouling: Is this what we wish to produce in a generation of children who are long on technical expertise but short on emotional depth, ethical passion, and transcendental longings always spurring them on to evolve in ways that will not only bring inner vision but also spur us all on to more capacious social vision and more courageous action to make that vision a reality, so that, together, we may attend to Lord Tennyson's thrilling injunction to "Come. 'Tis not too late to seek a newer world!"

In the end, the study of moral education is the ability to recognize that there are ethical absolutes in this world. Nuggets of "solids" that cannot be melted down by our understandable, even laudable, zeal to be tolerant towards all. But they are not culturally bound, these absolutes; they have nothing to do with pluralism, with diversity, with human rights. They are not "rights" at all; they are universal truths, the violations of which will cause great unhappiness and disequilibrium in the personal lives of the individual as well as the corporate lives of the community. But this distinction requires that we pay the piper—that we stop the counterintuitive assumptions about tolerance *ad infinitum.*

Postmodernism's overarching and overreaching ambition has been to undo *any* ethical structures within a culture as just an invention of one power-hungry "community of discourse" to lord it over another. This is the essence of *post*structuralism. In that vain and ultimately abortive project, we have forgotten the wisdom of such great structuralist as the anthropologist Claude Levi-Strauss, the Jesuit paleontologist Father Teilhard de Chardin, the cultural historian Jacques Barzun, and the pioneering psychologist Carl Jung that there are structures that inhere in any culture, are both ballast and propellants for that culture, and are, moreover, indispensable in grounding, maintaining, and advancing that culture. Without them, we are left—as the early 20th century poets and philosophers found themselves left—upon the shattered landscape of a world that has gone mad and become ill. The poet T.S. Eliot caught this world-historical malady with a desolate genius in that signature poem of the opening years of the 20th century, *The Wasteland,* where a morally relativistic culture is likened to a vexing vista of rootless, dead, or dying plants. In a passage that alludes to Ezekiel's vision of another such culture anciently that had failed to tend to its ethical roots, Eliot wrote:

> What are the roots that clutch, what branches grow
> Out of this stony rubbish? Son of man,
> You cannot say, or guess, for you know only
> A heap of broken images, where the sun beats,
> And the dead tree gives no shelter, the cricket no relief,
> And the dry stone no sound of water. . . .
> I will show you something different from either
> Your shadow at morning striding behind you
> Or your shadow at evening rising to meet you;
> I will show you fear in a handful of dust. (1971, 135)

With most things that come along in life, we must be tolerant. But with a few things, we must categorically demand their inclusion in society as indispensable norms. And, with a few things, we must categorically demand their exclusion, such as racism. Taken together, these things comprise the law. The key, then, is in restoring what I call a 10–80–10 balance: 10% absolutely needed, 80% relatively accepted, and 10% absolutely abhorred. We have concentrated much of our time and energy in the past 50 plus years on the shaded area between the second and third categories—that is, in securing the line between what is relatively accepted and what is absolutely abhorred. Now it is time to examine and to secure the boundary between the first and second categories, between what we absolutely need and what we can relatively accept. Then, and only then, we will restore happiness to the people, because the pillars of the American faith will have been repaired.

From that restored house, moral education will be a very reachable goal in the world of public education, understood fully by people as to its place and its role in America.

But where can we find this "American Faith" that the great majority of Americans will find not only tolerable but that will actually generate a new vision of America that can carry us forward? For this, I turn to early- to mid-twentieth century scholarship, when the idea of a tolerant but solid sense of some sorts of ethical universals was not taboo, as it has become in the dispiriting fare that postmodernism has heaped upon our engorged plates in its dazzling but ethically devastating documents. Combining ideas from Dewey's A Common Faith (1934), Will Herberg's Protestant, Catholic, Jew (1954), Daniel Bell's (1976) *The Cultural Contradictions of Capitalism*, and Martin Buber's (1965) *I and Thou,* I would like to propose the following ideas as comprising the heart of basic of such a faith.

First, from Dewey' *A Common Faith*, there is the notion that democracy is a group of individuals, each in pursuit of the highest good as he knows it, and that each one of these individuals has the right to do this so long as his idea of his personal self-realization does not infringe upon others. For Dewey, such individuals in deep, meaningful, compassionate communion each other as, together, they form questions and devise answers to move them forward as individuals and a society—this is democracy. The new American faith must restate and reclaim this virtue, this balance between a system that privileges only the individual as in *laissez faire* capitalism, on one hand, and one that privileges only the collective with no or little sense of the needs and rights of the individual, on the other hand, characterizes communism. In accomplishing this, society, especially its schools, must educate the child into the virtues of tolerance, the dynamics of balance, and the responsibility to keep this grand democratic experiment called democracy moving forward toward higher levels of consciousness and creativity.

The problem with this Deweyan vision is that it lacks the action of the Divine—or at least, the hope of it—in the operation of the state and in its vision of its future. This is a point that Bell makes in *The Cultural Contradictions of Capitalism.* It is all very well to talk about the centrality of the individual in a political economy, but we must realize, he warns, that there are two competing understandings of "the individual" in the American experience. The first is the idea, taken from Enlightenment philosophy, that the individual has the right to maximize his ability to express and himself and to structure things so as to always be enhancing his access to what he considers pleasurable. This privileges what Bell calls "expressive/utilitarian" idea of what it means to be an "individual." The role of government here is simply to make sure that no one's rights are violated in the process. By definition, this is not a point of view that leads to the kind of compassion, conversation and interpersonal commitment that we looked at above as key to a viable "common faith."

But all is not lost, says Bell, for there is a second, competing form of "the philosophy of the individual" in Western culture. It is rooted in the notion that the individual is important because she or he was made "in the image of God." The assumption that God is an individual and a person, albeit a supremely exalted one, is precisely what gives each human being's existence its unique ethical and ontological value. And there is more. For, since every individual is a child of this personal God, each one must treat others and be treated by them not only in a legally correct way but in a philosophically sound, emotionally deep, and ethically committed way. A system of government designed to promote that end, is, Bell says, a *Republic*. And the God who oversees this is precisely the God of the Bible—Author of the Judeo-Christian ethic. This form of "individualism" Bell, therefore, calls "Biblical-Republican" individualism. In comparing Expressive/Utilitarian individualism with Biblical/Republican individualism, Bell clearly sees the latter as superior to the former in most ways and certainly as a foundation of "a common faith." However, we must also allow room for the former since it is the engine of industrial and postindustrial production under the sign of the dollar.

What is more, this common faith, agreeable to Catholic, Protestant, and Jew, will both reflect and synthesize the confluence of the three major religions in America into a sort of generic religiosity that is agreeable to most Americans. For as Herberg notes in his work, it is not only possible but historically natural, even inevitable, that Americans would look for a religious orientation that would synthesize the general elements of each one while saving for its own places of worship and keeping out of public discourse and shared action those theological precepts and religious practices that are unique to it. It not only can but must accomplish all of this without insisting on the primacy of one of the religious worldviews. Although the question becomes more complex with the introduction of Islam into the mix for reasons which it is beyond the scope of this book and the expertise of its author to go into, there is still nothing in principle that would keep this salubrious synthesis from happening even with Islam as part of the implicit "Divine" in our new political economy.

None of this can happen, of course, without civilized discourse, which is the lifeblood of any democratic process. Indeed, what is democracy, if it is operating well, but an ongoing conversation? In this perpetual conversation, citizens hammer out answers to complex questions, resulting in compromise views that spur the nation on to further development, ever more consequential questions, and an ever deeper and higher commitment to this world-historically unique form of self-governance and collective growth. This is where Martin Buber's idea of the ethical as being tantamount to engaging in capacious and generous discourse with her dialogical "other" comes into play.

Putting this all together, we come up with a vision of a common faith as: 1) a balance between the legitimate claims of the individual and the collective, 2) a generic monotheistic ethic, which, not insisting upon the individual's subscribing to any of those religions, can thereby serve as the ethical foundation of the new American society, but one that does not privilege a particular faith tradition but does wish to function in the light of some sort of Divine guidance that touches the soul of every human being, 3) a commitment to humane *I and Thou* political discourse with fellow citizens as "dialogical partners" in order to honor the wisdom in each other's point of view—to teach and to learn, each one of us, in the dialectics of democracy, and 4) a Biblical-Republican understanding of the individual as our primary point of ethical reference but with commonsensical Utilitarian /Expressive individualism as the economic level of it all.

This can happen by means of the schools. Indeed, it must. Schools must become places where these capabilities are discussed, enacted, nurtured, and embedded in every aspect of the curriculum and every relationship on campus. I call this "education in the light of a common faith."

Just as I have argued that a paradigm shift is necessary in terms of the ethics of education, I want now to make another suggestion for a paradigm shift in the epistemology of American education. By epistemology, of course, I am referring to that branch of philosophy that deals not so much with *what* we know but rather with *how* we know. It is concerned with the processes of knowing. One would think that educational theorists would take a lively interest in epistemology since the curriculum is, or should be, all about "processes of knowing." More typically, however, teachers tend to accept the curriculum they are given to teach or settle into the one they have personally constructed over the years, and this they do without generally asking: "What assumptions am I making about *how* students come to know something? I often ask myself *what* the student should know, but too rarely do I ask myself *how* they come to know." In the section that follows, I would like to turn an epistemological lens to curriculum and instruction in order to see what epistemological assumptions we tend to operate off of in schooling and to suggest radically new ones. Indeed, I am calling for a "paradigm shift" in the epistemology of education in the U.S. no less fundamental than the one I have just called for in the ethics of education.

By the way, the term "paradigm shift" has been thrown around quite a bit since it was coined by physicist and historian of science Thomas Kuhn about 50 years ago in his highly influential study *The Structure of Scientific Revolutions*. But how exactly did Kuhn define a paradigm shift? Wrote Kuhn:

> In its established usage, a paradigm is an acceptable model or pattern . . . the paradigm functions by permitting the replication of examples any one of which could in principle serve to replace it. In a science, on the other hand, paradigm is rarely an object for replication. Instead, like an accepted judicial decision in common law, it is an object for further articulation and specification under new or more stringent conditions. (Kuhn 1970, 23)

The paradigm for the world of American education has been to go with the mind as the source of learning, rather than also with the heart. The Thinking-Sensates of the Meyers-Briggs Personality Inventory are the winners over the Feeling-Intuitives. Reason, not revelation, is the name of the game in schools. The problem with this mode of curriculum creation and delivery is that it fails to take into account something that is every bit as important as the "objective curriculum." It is "the subjective curriculum," which refers to each student's unique inner experience of the curriculum. For some students, the curriculum is a delight, for others a horror, and for most it is something in between. But in each and every case, the student's feelings about what she is learning are as relevant to the process of learning as are her thoughts about it. Indeed, negative feelings about what is being learned can subvert, twist, and downright destroy whatever the teacher is trying to get across in strictly objective terms. In other words:

> In psychodynamic terms, the student inevitably brings to a topic of study in the classroom her already existing *complex* of ideas, feelings, experiences, associations and even somatic responses regarding that topic. This is what is meant by the "subjective curriculum' and it is never the same for any two students. [This] will involve a student's hopes and fears, attractions and repulsions, successes and failures. Her sense of the item's relevancy or irrelevancy to her lifeworld will come to bear on her engagement with a curricular item, and this will be organically tied into her family's and culture's feelings on the topic, the political

and ethical voltage the item has for them. In general, the question always arises about what symbolic associations and other subconscious processes Topic A might set off in the student from the very start. All of these factors, and so many more, all put together, account for the extreme importance of the subjective curriculum. They explain why a "simple though'" in the classroom is never simple, just as it is never simple in a consulting room. It is complex. Indeed, it is *a complex.* In fact, every thought is. There has probably never been a completely objective thought since our specie started having them. For this reason, we must come to see that cognition is not a cold affair of simple ratiocination. Cognition is "hot"—heated by many passions, commitments, fears, ideals, historical traumas and future hopes. (Mayes 2020, 176)

What does all this mean? It means that the complete curriculum will see the students as a complete being—not simply a *cognizing* being but also a *feeling* being, and that this is natural and healthy. Indeed, it answers to our two epistemological capacities, as we have already seen in our brief discussion of Kant. Those two capacities are the *mathetic/analytical* and the *poetic/intuitional.* According to Kant, neither way is superior to the other. They are simply the two ways that we know ideas, things, and other people, and that one without the other opens the door to problems that will issue from the neglected domain. Neglect the emotional domain, and students will justifiably begin to resist material in the merely theoretical mode. But neglect the analytical, and students will soon either reject the curriculum because of its sloppy sentimentalism or get lost in that sentimentalism. In this, as in all things, balance is key. And this is the paradigm shift I am advocating for: An equal valorizing of the cognitive and the emotional, the syllogistic and the poetic.

How necessary is such a sea-change, such a paradigm shift? Just listen to the cry of the ones who have left the system in the past 45 years—both the liberal homeschoolers and the conservative evangelical Christians. In short, matters for the mind might very well be the carbohydrates of education, but habits of the heart could very well be the protein needed for the long-term sustenance for the growing child.

To be more practical, the reforms, as well as the money spent these past decades, were much ado about technology for the classroom, that is, about the method of delivery of the instruction. Indeed, the reforms all stemmed from the same paradigm.

Normal science consists in the actualization of [the promise of success discoverable in selected and still incomplete examples], an actualization achieved by extending the knowledge of those facts that the paradigm displayed as particularly revealing by increasing the extent of the match between those facts and the paradigms predictions, and by further articulation of the paradigm itself. (Kuhn 1970, 24)

For the 2020's to be truly successful in the implementations of the reforms the past two generations, our paradigm must not be allowed to be refined yet again. Rather, it must be challenged to its core. And what needs to occur is nothing short of a once-per-century overhaul. Kuhn points the way for such an outing, one that will involve a radical reexamining and reformulation of the aims and shapes of the new, more holistic curricula—those that do not just move along the same cognitivist lines into more and more elaborately articulated versions of them but that also dare to venture in directions—thinking thoughts, imagining possibilities, challenging conventional wisdom—in ways that make education more enjoyable, more truly democratic, and more likely to produce true innovation and advantage to American society. What Kuhn writes of professional scientific inquiry holds equally true for any process of inquiry that happens within the schools, too. He thus highlights problems in the epistemology of public education just as relevantly and trenchantly as he does problems in the doing of normative science when he writes:

> Closely examined . . . that enterprise seems an attempt to force nature into the preformed and relatively inflexible box that the paradigm supplies. No part of the aim of normal science is to call forth new sorts of phenomena; indeed, those that will not fit into the box are often not seen at all. Nor do scientists normally aim to invent new theories and they often are intolerant of those invented by others. Instead, normal scientific research is directed to the articulation of those phenomena and theories that the paradigm already supplies. (Kuhn 24–25)

Perhaps we have done really well this past century in seeking quantitative success. Certainly, it is so much easier to measure. Science has led the way, as progress has been measured faithfully and quite accurately. But, I will propose here, where we have failed has been not just in acting upon significant and well-understood qualitative measures, but even more so in securing and debating philosophical queries (that is, the asking of timely and powerful questions). Music and art have retreated into a corner, whereby progress has been measured with how accurately these fields have imitated life rather than contributing a unique inspiration to life. Even history has become bogged down into a hunt for ever-increasingly smaller bits of minutiae rather than any significant tie-ins between generations, between nations, or between centuries.

What I would like to offer now, therefore, is a very general view of what I believe most of us would agree to as being appropriate goals for education to accomplish at a pace that most of us know or can easily imagine. Still, it does require a bit of "going back to the drawing board" to get a clear picture from the get-go of what I am about here. I will elaborate on this picture as we move along. Thus, to begin, allow me to unveil this first preliminary canvas:

to the drawing boards we must go. To begin, let us bring up a canvas which we all can recognize. I am not claiming that U.S. education has necessarily accomplished all of these goals on this schedule, but I am suggesting that a consensus may be assumed about the desirability of this content at this developmental pace.

GRANDPARENTING: BEING PATIENT TO LEARN

After the fourth year of teaching high school upperclassmen and concerned with their struggle to become successful students in the required US Government, Economics and American history courses, I began to notice that I was offering the following piece of advice rather frequently: "Read, think, write, ask questions, and, above all, be patient." That seemed to be the best path for students to take if they wanted to go the distance with their demanding teacher. I have come to realize that this little reminder had much more significant ramifications than simple advice for those 11th graders. And now that I have this extraordinary privilege, once again, after a 32-year absence, of teaching 11th grade U.S. history this year as well as Dual Credit U.S. history, (albeit in a rather different zip code, let alone area code!), I find myself offering my best advice in the form of three 3-word sentences: "Find your voice. Gain your vision. Write your script." Each one of these morsels wound up being a crucial ingredient in my own lifelong educational journey. And hopefully in a few thousand students, from both then and now.

So, what I propose is a very generalized plan of what, when all is said and done, goes on (or is hoped to go on) at different levels of an American education currently. Cognitively, the second-grader is in the process of, as many elementary school teachers have told me, learning to read. It is a key step to take; successful completion will allow the child to attempt the other half of his or her assignment in the primary years: reading to learn. By the fifth grade, or what has become the final year in elementary school, the child should be completing this process. With this first rung completed, the child has begun the five-tiered climb towards a successful cognitive education.

For the secondary school student, his/her task is to grapple with thinking. If the boy's or girl's middle school experience has been successful, at least intellectually, he/she has learned skills in how to think by the end of 8th grade: whether first by memory, or later (as Bloom's Taxonomy famously reminds us), by comprehension, application, analysis, synthesis or even evaluation. The student is on the way towards acquiring a second set of tools by which to learn. By the end of 11th grade, the young man or woman should have been challenged to the point that he/she has now gained some facility with the art of thinking to learn. With the rung successfully mastered, further tools for a

Table 3.2. The 5 tiers and transitions in educational processes

1st Tier: Primary Education
K–Grade 1: Transitioning
Grade 2: Learning to Read
Grades 3–4: Consolidation/Transitioning
Grade 5: Reading to Learn
Grade 6: Consolidation/Transitioning

2nd Tier: Secondary Education
Grade 7: Consolidation/Transitioning
Grade 8: Learning to Think
Grades 9–10: Consolidation/Transitioning
Grade 11: Thinking to Learn
Grade 12: Consolidation/Transitioning

3rd Tier: Higher Education (Undergraduate)
Freshman-Sophomore: Learning to Write
Junior-Senior: Writing to Learn

4th Tier: Higher Education (Graduate)
Masters: Learning to Ask Effective Questions
Doctorate: Asking Effective Questions to Learn

5th Tier: Parenting Education (or, "The Art of Sacrifice")
Parenting: Learning to be Patient

successful education await him/her at the university. Still, we must remember that this first phase focuses solely upon the area of cognitive growth.

For many Americans, formal education stops here and directly proceeds to what I have labeled the 5th tier. While this is not a criticism of those who cannot or who choose not to proceed to the 3rd or 4th tiers of higher education, one must certainly recognize that, if higher education does succeed with its missions (in the realms of writing and of asking effective questions), then the non-college-bound student does miss out. Until recently, many Americans have realized the potential gain for their education by desiring to attend college, in seeking that additional tier or two.

At the college level, writing should be paramount, regardless of the expected major. Whether in the first language of the institution, whether in code, whether in diagrams, this is a must. Underclassmen struggle with learning what the professor wants from them. Often, and for a large percentage of the average high school graduates, it is the young adult's first major experience with lengthy writing. If the student's underclass experience has been successful, then he/she should have gained success with learning to write. In the junior and senior year, the student, now having declared a major, should find him/herself ready and able to write in order to learn, whether it be the lab report, the complex mathematical proof, the five-page short story or the lengthy research paper. A third tier of cognitive education will have been reached.

One word about the community college or the trade school student: technical or what we improperly call "vocational" education is generally not concerned with mastery of this third tier. The tech student *does* gain training, ostensibly for profitable employment. But this is not to be confused with gaining an education, which is meant to broaden rather than to focus. Tools and skills are linked with training; intellect and cognition are linked with education.

In passing, it is important to note the rather more cynical but still important interpretation of the real, and not-so cheery visions of the role of community colleges, which Karabel and Halsey call their "cooling down" hypothesis. By this view, community colleges are cheap ways for kids—still largely white and middle class—who have been primed for their entire lives to go to a four-year college, to finish their first two years of general requirements inexpensively and conveniently. From there they jump up to the four-year institution as juniors in good standing and ready to rumble academically.

However, for poorer students, often rural white and urban young people of color, the two-year-degree is often in a "field" that is merely technical and will not gain them much more than perhaps a bit more pay in a field they would have probably gone into anyway, and, with or without the A.A. degree, one in which they are not bound to advance very far in the field anyway. Statistics show, too, that students from lower socioeconomic strata do not tend to enroll in strictly academic subjects. Nevertheless, having received an "AA degree" creates in them what Marx called "the false consciousness" that they have now had higher education and that the system has served them, whereas, in fact, it simply fools them into thinking that things are substantially different and that they have and have attained things that they are not and have not. This prevents them from recognizing the social injustice of which they are victims and to blame themselves when (mysteriously!) their condition winds up being not very different from their friends who did not go to a community college, which has served merely to "cool down" their expectations and leave the system of socioeconomic oppression unchanged.

Although Karabel and Halsey may overstate the case, they still raise an important point about this branch of "higher education" that began in the early 20th century and has never really risen to the liberatory potential it promised for people who come from social climes that did not prepare them for truly efficacious higher education. According to Karabel and Halsey, it still does not.

For many four-year college graduates, technical or vocational training now beckons, whether in the confines of a corporation, as an apprentice in a small business venture, or in the classrooms of the law, the business, or the medical school. For many, adult education awaits them in the near future as they begin dailies of their own. But, for some, there exists the increasingly rare opportunity to proceed to graduate school in the arts or the sciences to gain competence at the fourth tier: learning to ask the big questions and asking big questions to learn. These are those who will occupy the most prestigious, top 10% of the global workforce, "symbolic analysts," according to President Clinton's Secretary of Labor Robert Reich (1991) in his then-instant classic *The Work of Nations*. The other, less prestigious and considerably less well paid workers are, in rank order from top to bottom: lower-level administrators, teachers and government workers, factory workers with routine work but with important life and health benefits, and in-service workers, the most precariously positioned workers who labor in such places as fast-food restaurants, chain motels performing largely menial tasks, and with few or no benefits to protect them against the all-too-real daily possibilities of illness and accidents.

Back to near the top of the pecking order: Masters' degree students generally find themselves overwhelmed, as the tricks they learned as undergraduates seem no longer to hold them above water. Complaints rifle off of classroom walls, as similar-looking professors with the obligatory button-down look or, alternately, the "tenured-radical" jeans and rough-hewn/pricey shirt, rattle them with new and more complex assignments. The assignments for papers seem more and more vague. Students crave for predetermined topics and clear-cut syllabi, which instead challenge them for the need for much greater self-starting on their part on course papers or projects. The fledgling graduate student gropes for a while as he/she has done before at the lower tiers, trying to find the keys for success. Probably (and only after some time beyond graduation), the skill that the professor was subtly trying to instill in the student becomes apparent: *Learning to ask questions.*

It is precisely this, above all else, that is the skill which, if all goes well in graduate school, the student will garner and cultivate. These invaluable skills gained at this level, which tend to appear more with the M.A. and the M.S. rather than the more formulaic professional degrees of an M.B.A or the M.Ed., is what prepares the graduate student to become an innovator and leader in the community.

With doctoral work, asking questions to learn becomes the #1 skill and the quintessential component of competence. Coursework becomes a warm-up for the real purpose at the end of this fourth tier: finding and directing one's own equation, usually in the form of a dissertation, so that the asking of questions has taken hold, and has been imbued with a life of its own. Interestingly enough, the process that began at the very outset of tier one has been completely reversed: the students, formerly answering the teacher's questions, now become the student who asks his own questions. He becomes a scholar, a mover and shaker, a break-free and breakaway thinker, who not only asks the hard questions but raises questions that few if any have thought of before.

The fifth tier has become more difficult to master in this age of the "now" and in what Christopher Lasch (1991) has called "The Culture of Narcissism." In a culture of narcissism, such as our own, much revolves in crazy idiosyncratic orbits from person to person about *my* projects, *my* lifestyle, *my* fashion choices, *my* upward mobility, *my* glorious career, *my* mixed portfolio, *my* latest trip to *my* condo, and *my* (most recent) lover. Where is the sense of the Other whom one serves in lovely, simple, and spiritual acts of service, sacrifice, and self-surrender? We run off to therapy at the drop of a hat. But how many of our maladies stem from a life lived in such self-absorption that we never partake of the healing elixir of giving of oneself to others and even to duty itself? We do well to remember the lines from the Roman poet Seneca which Wordsworth uses as the epigram to his poem. Wrote Seneca: "I am no longer good through deliberate intent, but by long habit have reached a point where I am not only able to do right, but am unable to do anything but what is right." (Seneca, Letters 120.10)

The existential education of parenting is, in its origin, its purpose, and its necessity, key in our holistic growth. It is duty, which, along with its challenges, yields a special spiritual sustenance to upbuild the soul of the person who cares enough about others to do his duty to the, for it is in the love of God and others that we first apprehend and then carry out those blessed acts, which, because they are not *about* ourselves are so morally sustaining and expanding *to* ourselves.

Besides, instead of quite so many hours of therapy in which we take, take, take, how healing would we find it to spend a few of those hours giving, and in the process learning to enter into others' suffering and do something to lessen their loads—all the while realizing how relatively light our load actually is by way of comparison.

Rather, the overly-opulent, finally rather silly opera of Narcissism consists of just one insipid note: "Me! Me! Me!" This is not an integrated life, for there can be no life that is truly rich in all of its existential domains and facets that is not thickly landscaped with the organic life of service.

Just before he died, the great British journalist and devout Catholic Malcolm Muggeridge wrote a book entitled *Something Beautiful for God* (1971). Parenting and grandparenting—or symbolic variations on it through any number of charitable organizations that welcome volunteers with open arms—offer rare opportunities to work, in the deepest love, towards just that existentially gorgeous end that Muggeridge is pointing us towards by the very title of his book. And let us bear in mind, too, that most teachers do not become teachers for the pay (which is not a great deal) or prestige (rather, they are the symbolic whipping-boy for all of society's ills that it would rather not face about itself but would rather export them to teachers). No. Most teachers become teachers because of the opportunity to be of service to children and to better the communities in which they live, move and have their being.

To make this point. Let us return to Daniel Bell's (1976) *The Cultural Contradictions of Capitalism,* briefly discussed above. You will recall that the distinction was drawn between a form of individualism that is anathema to democracy and another form of it that lies at the very heart of democracy. On one hand, expressive/utilitarian individualism is all about the ego, maximizing its insatiable appetites, feeding its vapid vanity, consolidating a culture of narcissism that only parades around as democracy but is not. On the other hand, "biblical, republican" individualism is all about protecting the civil rights, emotional well-being, and ethical stature of the individual. The former wallows in self-indulgence. The latter liberates self and others in service. This is what I mean by patience and the virtue of "Parenting Education." It does not require being an actual biological parent. It does require having deep paternal and maternal care for one's fellow beings.

At this level of psychological, ethical, and spiritual development, the true student attempts to bolster any and all of his/her former education. The skill asks for the mastery of something that is essential to a high-level quality of life. For any who have forgotten the importance of the quality of patience, recall the fascination that both young and old had with the Star Wars' character named Yoda. Of course, for those who are familiar with Eastern thought, this emphasis on patience will come as no surprise. And so, one's cognitive or "traditional" education continues as a parent.

There is no doubt that the curriculum for "learning to be patient" might take a bit longer to complete than college courses do! Indeed, it would be a contradiction in terms if patience could be learned on the cheap and on the run. It takes time. But, with some hard work, as well as working through the challenges that life imposes upon all of us, gradual successes are not only attainable but quite requisite to one's evolution as a human being. In this sense, the one level of education that is not in any way "required" and is not even though of as "education" proper, is, from a more spiritual perspective that takes the entire sweep of our mortal run into account, the most significant education we will ever engage in.

Finally, the lesson of patience once again becomes possible as one enters the world of grandparenthood. No longer too close to see clearly, the grandparent has the latitude to enjoy a slower pace of life; being patient seems to foster insights as well as joys in coming to grips with the cognitive circle of life, now nearing its completion. Carl Jung was the first psychologist in the modern Western tradition to look at midlife and beyond as developmentally significant and not just a sort of sad loss of all the obvious potentialities of youth as one stumbled towards death. Rather, he viewed the second half of life as rich and uniquely empowered in its own way—and ways that could contribute to the evolution of a culture in deeper wisdom, not just the maintenance of culture in uncritical youthful ambition.

The grand model now appears one-third complete. What I mean by that is that I have dealt now with the very broad contours of traditional education in the *cognitive* domain. This *cognitive domain* has been revealed and arranged in the form of a ladder.

Our attention must now turn to two other domains that, while not as apparent as the first one, still command our attention as we come to recognize their place in the true curriculum—that is, the curriculum that addresses all the domains of our existence, the holistic curriculum (Forbes 2003, Mayes 2019). Let us invoke Bloom's old but still very useful characterization of these next two domains as the affective and the psychomotor curricula. As part of the null curriculum, whoever the curriculum writer, although athletic coaches might wince at my insistence that psychomotor education be labeled as "hidden."

Perhaps they are well aware of this education and have the curricula written up and posted up inside of Google Classroom. Nevertheless, I still strongly suggest that many educators are neglectful of the contribution of this segment of the faculty. Such a statement might beg further research. But, the next domain of the grand model awaits our inspection.

Returning to the model's arrangement, we can see once again the inclusion of the grade level and the level of skill that needs to be attained. The second domain, then, looks at the affective aspect of the complete education that I am advocating for.

For the 2nd grader, school allows for all sorts of occasions in learning how to listen: from the silence required on the way to the lunchroom, to the silence demanded during nap time; from the silence expected from all when one is called upon in class, to the silence observed when the teacher is making the individual rounds. The 5th grader finds him/herself listening to the sound of waves in science class as well as listening to a speech given by Martin Luther King in social studies class. A successful primary education in this domain has focused upon and sharpened the youngster's auditory facility, a facility that will serve him/her well as he/she enters middle or junior high school.

At the second tier, the student begins the painful task of learning to identify what puberty is quickly screaming about: getting in touch with the emotions. It is certainly an education to be had—one with the help of trained teachers and patient parents, who between the two, might offer ample expertise. But with hard work, the wild years of pubescence yield to the challenging times of adolescence. High school students are now confronted with more demands on their time and on their confidence. Still, having successfully negotiated the pitfalls of a confusing 7th and 8th grade by learning to identify these blossoming and powerful emotions, the teen is now ready to learn from this array of new equipment.

Indeed, under the pull of Freudian developmental psychology, the middle school was created as precisely the place that would help students transition through this developmentally crucial yet also highly perilous 7th and 8th grade years, to prepare her for the rough and tumble of high school (Watras 2002). The kind of emotional Identification with one's specific religioethical and socioeconomic subcultures-of-origin must now give way to integration; enunciation must lead to elaboration. The 11th grader attains a successful affective education when he/she can make such a successful transition in the use of this new emotional adroitness and force in concert with his cognitive structures and attainments. That, at least, is the historical origin and ideological justification for the existence of the middle school.

Rarely is there time in the high school for the average student to verbalize more than a few utterances of agreement or of quick identifications back to the teacher. This must change if the next tier of education is to be attempted in this domain. Learning to speak up takes place in all sorts of settings for the college student. It might be in small sections of the large introductory courses; it might take place in the student cafeteria; it might occur as a member of one of the campus clubs or organizations. The point, though, is that learning to speak is the crucial next step in this domain.

By the end of one's undergraduate days (and again, this education is not taken by all young adults), speaking up should have become the prime accomplishment in the field of affective education. With this skill, it becomes much easier to gain a sense of where one stands in the rein of ideas: where on the political spectrum does one lie? Where in the debate on an international crisis between the U.S. and China does one stand? What does one believe concerning the return of the Messiah? All sorts of ideas can be sorted out with a successful competence in the art of elocution.

As the French saying goes, "Plus ça change, plus c'est la même chose": "The more things change, the more they remain the same." There is nothing new under the sun. And certainly, these ideas that I have been laying out—although meant to be fitted to current conditions, circumstances, and hopes—still hearken back to ancient Greek education, in which expert facility with grammar and rhetoric were two of the most important goals of a broad education. What I aim, at least in part, to accomplish here is to highlight the continuity, over more than two thousand years, of what comprises a good and solid education.

In graduate work, active skills yield to more passive ones. At first blush, this statement may strike the reader as counterintuitive, given the considerably more extensive reading and essay-writing that college requires of the student, even greater than the last two years of high school. But consider. In a university system, where the student is lectured to all day by authorities in their fields (although, alas, that authority is too often more self-proclaimed than actual) the student is called upon to attend scrupulously to everything the teacher says, especially when that grade hangs on how well the student can, on a test, regurgitate back to the professor that professor's opinions about this or that. This is not to say that there are not professors, and many of them, who know and love their fields well.

It is to say, however, that in trying to get to the truth of a matter, the university student needs to have her radar constantly up for what of truth and what of self-serving speculation is issuing from the professor's lectern—and how to discern the difference. This also requires close-listening and that hones the student's ability to discern statements that are reliable from those that may sound reliable but are actually specious. Interestingly, many professors have learned that with the advent of the web and instant access to information, they must be much more careful about truth-claims that they make, for those claims may easily be researched and tested in the blink of an eye by students sitting behind their open computers.

Interestingly, this might seem strikingly similar to the developmental task of the 8-year-old, who is also enjoined by the teacher to "listen carefully to what I say and be sure that you do it." But it is much more a procedural matter in the 3rd year classroom to listen carefully than it is an intellectual one, as in the graduate seminar.

That said, let us not forget Lipman's interesting approach to curricula in the elementary school years that revolve around his notion in *Philosophy Goes to School* (1988) that, when stated in developmentally-appropriate terms and emotionally-congruent contexts, students in the very youngest years can begin to grasp philosophical issues drawn from Plato, Aristotle, Spinoza and Kant. Thus, perhaps there is some symbolism—or at least the promise of a possibility for expanded elementary school curricula—in the return to the quiet that close-listening demands at whatever level of instruction.

Of course, in the doctoral seminar, there will be many more finely-tuned antennae up than just a pair of ears and eyes. But in both cases, *mutatis mutandi,* learning to observe encompasses the art of when to listen and when to speak, of when to express feelings and when not to. Learning to observe draws the student back out from his own needs and wants and refocuses them on the external world. And it is certainly true that the important fundamental distinction abides that the more advanced the curriculum, the more it requires the student (or at least, *should* require the student) to *decenter* from his little world, both geographically and ideologically, and expand his worldview by being less anxious to jump in with a personal opinion and more concerned about taking everything in before forming an opinion for public consumption in the first place. The first year of graduate work focuses greatly on this skill. That is why teachers, who have the luxury of taking a sabbatical have the privilege of stepping away from the torrid pace of 500–1000 interactions per day (second only, by the way, to air traffic controllers) may choose to step into this graduate school world of observing once again.

And here we come across what Marx called a "contradiction." It is when a society professes to believe one thing but acts in quite a different way. One of the great contradictions in U.S. society is, on one hand, all of our fine and fancy rhetoric about the nobility of the calling of being a teacher, and how little we pay teachers and how few paid released hours, days, or weekends we give them to spend in the library, go to conferences, or write essays and books in their fields, on the other hand. If teachers received twice the pay and had half the workload, they could do this, and it would redound to the benefit of the teachers and students alike. To those who say it would be too expensive to do such a thing, three or four fewer Stealth bombers in our already glutted military would probably cover the costs of such things nationwide quite nicely. This is a Marxian contradiction in our society. It is a grievous one. It drives many fine and gifted people from K-12 teaching or dissuades them from entering the field in the first place. Who suffers from this? Everyone!

Back to the theme of affective education, however, one does suspect the possibility that an affective education may be gained outside the gates of a university. And finally, the parent learns to exercise his/her will, usually as a result of a child's demands upon that will. Growing children provide the perfect education for that will: when to use it, when not to use it, and when to let go and allow the child free agency. It is a wonderful gift that demands that the parents continue their existential and moral education in listening, patience, the courageous use of their wills and the wisdom when to curb that will in the greater interest of the child. Failure to do so would result in not only a poor education, but poor parenting, with all its ramifications. Grandparenting is the icing on the cake, in its call to be willing to learn.

The third domain must now be explored, although its components seem more difficult to secure a sure grasp on. For this reason, I will collapse the grade levels into "primary education," "secondary education," "higher education undergraduate," "higher education graduate" and "Parenting/ Grandparenting education." Perhaps those athletic coaches can contribute to this model in the future research hinted at above. Nevertheless, the domain must be presented, for, here the qualities of a psychomotor education take shape. Once again, a reminder is in order—namely, that the grand model is for a system's *potential*, and not to be confused with any local *reality*.

For the elementary school student, fundamental motor skills are of prime concern. In addition, rudimentary starts with balance, agility, dexterity, litheness and strength should be sought. Learning about the individual motor apparatus seems to be the order of the day (or actually of six years of days), whether for use in individual recreation or in competitive sports. For the secondary school student, physical development should keep up with physical growth. Unfortunately, too much energy tends to be spent in explaining what is happening to the body in the form of a health class or even an anatomy class. In an increasingly litigious society, we have become gun-shy of taking the education to the fields and letting the "fingers [and the toes] do the walking," rather the mouth do the talking. But, continued education should be possible in the form of better coordination skills, increased knowledge and experience in sports and games, and development of stronger bone marrow and muscle tissue.

The college student is, for the most part, asked to assume the responsibility for the continuity and the integration of his physical education into his/her busy schedule. Except for a few universities that hold onto a physical education requirement for the freshman, the facilities are all there for the potential use of the student. But, the "curriculum" is geared for the intercollegiate athlete; the collars certainly follow that curriculum. What has begun here is the emergence of a null curriculum, or of an education that is neither stated nor implied. It is to be found only with a good deal of searching and discipline. Granted, the facilities exist, sometimes of the highest quality for any interested students. Of course, for the graduate student, this education becomes even more elusive. It is not expected of him or her to continue (let alone to progress), and oftentimes, the facilities are not available to the per-credit tuition paying graduate student. This notion of a null curriculum becomes more apparent.

Before we move on to more serious implications for the null curriculum, it is time to summarize. What I have tried to chart has been the various domains of an education that are available to all, in varying degrees and in vastly varying qualities. It is not within the scope of this work to examine these variations. Rather it is intended that the domains be examined as a whole for correctness as well as completeness. Thus, with Figure we see in the graphic immediately below the integration of the domains held for a broad level of education. Reading, listening, and gaining fundamental motor skills is the work in the primary grades. Thinking, feeling, and greater physical control are the work on the secondary grades. In the world of higher education, the college or university does not claim to have a monopoly over this domain. And for the adult, there should come a "healthy" acceptance of the decreasing abilities of the body, of the diminishing strikes that can be taken over the duration of mortal life. Allowing for these changing abilities will add much to the wisdom of the human being in this domain.

We have come far in our search for a completed landscape. What we have examined, it seems, is the search to be both smart, happy, and coordinated. But we have not addressed the second part of Plato's maxim that "the point of education is to become smart and to become good." Three domains have not given us what we are searching for. Thus, moral education becomes our next pallet, the fourth domain.

If there is one thread to hold onto as we enter the next domain, it is that of the null curriculum, or that part of the curriculum that is neither explicitly nor implicitly taught. It is the piece of curriculum that, for one reason or another, is overlooked, avoided, or even denied. Moral education is a stinging example of this null curriculum, even more so that the small swatch uncovered in the psychomotor domain. Without a full appreciation of the same steps of progression that we have been using, the person desiring to become morally educated is flustered at best, denied at worst. And so, we proceed.

Chapter 4

Mapping the Journey of the Heart

Columbine. April 20, 1999. Hitler's birthday. Mine as well. I believe I am wrapped into this work a little tighter than I might have expected. But such is the nature of deep personal reflectivity that the journey takes us much more than we take the journey.

Let me begin what will prove to be a statement of my ethical *Credo* by examining three statements from what the New York Times reported within five Sundays after that outbreak of evil at Columbine.

First, From Patrice Doyle: I do not believe I will ever understand what those horrible boys were thinking. That is what bugs me the most—what were they thinking? . . . (May 23, 1999).

Second, "There is a simple way to address school shootings: eliminate access to guns," said Dr. Alfred Blumstein. "Guns . . . transform what is widespread teen-age-behavior into disasters" (May 9, 1999).

Third, "Dr. James Comer, the Yale University psychiatrist has been saying for years that schools only address the intellectual needs of children and not their psychological and developmental ones. The current wave of school reform, with its relentless reliance on standard tests results, only makes things worse" (May 2, 1999).

In the weeks I have had to think about how exactly a decade's worth of research can bear fruit—a pile full of doodles on backs of airplane napkins, of writings every which way on gobs of legal pads, and all over not one but two large white boards might relate to these stunningly out of touch reactions on cable news—I find myself writing opening salvos in response to their partial-sightedness and shortsidedness:

Patrice, how can you possibly *not* understand what they were thinking? Indeed, what was going on in those boys was not about thinking. Primarily, it was about feeling, or the lack thereof. Second, are you not aware that there exists a clear and present danger in our secular society, and it is that it doesn't want to hear about such "outmoded" ideas as "good" and "evil" and even less does it want to hear that both principles are constantly fighting for predominance in the human heart? The danger lies in the fact that our blithe dismissal of this evil in the human heart makes it all the easier for that evil, unacknowledged and undealt with, to prevail. Finally, it is not a question of what these boys were thinking. It is a question of how timorously and inauthentically we approach the idea of good and evil in our lives in general and in our curricula.

Dr. Blumstein, how could you possibly miss the connection between guns and disasters—namely, that guns do not "transform" the perpetrator. Rather, they give him the "perfect" tool to put his evil into action. Guns do not *transform* who he is. They are the ultimate tool for him to *manifest* who he is! These feelings, or as I would assert, these loyalties to the dark forces, are so potent that to misunderstand, even deny, their depths (in favor of only seeing the weapon of choice to act out these feelings) is ethically and politically perilous, for, in denying the reality of evil, we but swing wide-open the door to its immediate manifestation and ultimate triumph. Let us be realistic, not politically correct, in recognizing the existence of evil, which ethical philosophers from Plato to Buber have asserted the ontological reality of with a resounding finality.

Dr. Comer, you are correct in lamenting how much schools fail to address children's psychological and developmental needs. But you neglect to mention how grievously they also fail to address the affective domain, let alone their utter disregard for the student's spiritual attunement. And while many including even Kevin Ryan, Thomas Lickona, and Alfie Cohn have spent careers writing about character education, some of us know that there are even deeper roots to tap than simply desirable behavioral shifts on the part of schoolchildren.

What these roots are about is the subject of this book. I now propose a theoretical model that might assist any individual who seeks to examine the amount of light he/she is operating under. And by light, I mean that which is good, pure, and of great worth. For many, light will also be connected with the "godly." By coming to grips with how much or how little light a person is living with, we can arrive at a solid alternative to what economics call the Rational Choice Theory. I call it the Emotional Disposition Theory. In other words, we are moving here beyond the limits of the merely "institutional curriculum" as defined by the state (Eisner and Vallance 1985) and venturing into the realm of the "subjective curriculum" (Mayes 2020) as it is received in the student's heart.

In this foray into the examinations of dispositions, we find that reason and rationality are stripped bare and—for all their undoubted importance—are shown up for what they *cannot* offer—namely, a complete picture of why the individual is disposed to do what he chooses to do. For it is only by conjoining the matters of the mind with the habits of the heart (and for some, the stirrings of the soul) that we find a clearer picture of why some who resort to a weapon seek to protect, and others who do the same seek to destroy. This work, in a nutshell, seeks to look more closely at human motivation, each one of us capable of just about anything, angelic or demonic. It is a matter of not only what we feel but where we find ourselves poised on many different situational planes of being, ranging from the familial to the historical as well as from the strictly personal to the more broadly spiritual.

FOUNDATIONAL PIECES

What is the individual's greatest desire in life? In most of our own lives' close encounters with others and painstaking examinations of ourselves, one comes to find that some desire great wealth, some fame, and others, power. Still others hope for meaningful relationships and meaningful work. Still others seek harmony, peace and tranquility. Even others seek draggable experiences through travel, sports, and recreation/leisure time. These desires draw from some of our highest intellectual, emotional or physical abilities. When all goes well, they attest to the joys of living in this world and in our mortal frames that carry us. Of course, all does not always go well in all of the domains of a person's existence, which is why holistic education is so important, for it allows the student to develop in areas that are, for one reason or another, problematic and will remain so, even morphing into a toxicity if left unattended that will finally poison the whole system.

However, far beyond the "carrots" and "sticks" of the capitalist system to motivate us to work, far deeper than the attractions of the physical world, higher than the soarings of the most intense personal emotions of love and hate, there remains a Timeless Force that billions upon this earth continue to hold dearest of all things and to which they happily, savingly even, invest with their deepest commitment. It is what the theologian Paul Tillich (1956) has called our "Ultimate Concern," no matter the name, tradition, and practices it goes by from person to person, place to place, time to time, or culture to culture.

While *It* remains indescribable for most, it is central to the entire existential functioning of those who hold to *It*. Moreover, we find that, invariably, in our efforts to work with people in the moral domain—not merely Bloom's cognitive, affective or psychomotor domains; for, this far transcends those—it demands that we tap Its immeasurable resources, yield to Its overwhelming power, and heed Its universal dictates, for it is these that lie at the very foundation of not only human life but all life. It is, as Rudolf Otto (1958) put it in his seminal but these days little-read work *The Holy,* the *mysterium tremendum et fascinans* ("the tremendous and fascinating mystery"). These are the true *resources* that lie at the foundations of all life and that overwhelm us with the *numinosum,* or the Spirit.

Of course, it is clear that many people are allured by the idea that the good of society is the ultimate standard of what constitutes ethical behavior—what Rosseau over three centuries ago called "the social contract" that we all presumably enter into simply by being members of a society. This notion still has a powerful presence today in ethical theory under the name of "social utilitarianism"—and it is the basis of what are called "social constructivist views of education" that dominate pedagogical theory currently—the idea that learning is primarily a social, not an individual, matter (Rogoff 1990). It is easy to see why this pragmatic and attractive emphasis on the good of society is the assumption from which many, if not indeed most people build their view of what is right and what is wrong. However, I wish to make it clear that in this study what is "good" does not rest primarily on the collective welfare as defined and measured by governmental agencies—although it admits the extreme importance of that—but begins, rather, with the individual.

For what is a society if not an aggregate of individuals? Society does not think a thought or have a feeling. The individual does. Besides, as Jung often insisted, if our focus is primarily on the needs of a society, we will inevitably wind up leading "an awful, grinding, banal life" in which we have been reduced to our social identity and utilitarian function in the society. This is simply an unnatural and counterintuitive way to live, Jung insists, for we are creatures who need to feel that we are part a "divine drama" and that without that feeling we will one day simply wither and die psychospiritually (Jung 1954, 274). Thus, the moral domain is situated primarily in and on the individual—his or her character. This refers to those inwardly developing attitudes that remain as hidden evidence of burgeoning dispositions in the individual to do right simply because that individual *intuits* that it is right, for it is, as Kant (1781/1997) put it, "a categorical imperative" that we are all born with by simple virtue of our humanity. And underlying this intuitive sense of what is right, there is also the equally profound sense within oneself that Deity *cares* that we do this "right," avoid what our deepest moral intuitions tell us is "wrong," and that we thereby please Deity.

I am aware that this is far from a popular idea in current academic discourse and that I will be labeled as naïve or an oppressor because I insist on the simplest but most universal features of a universal code of ethics. But the plain fact is that most people do believe in it, always have done, always will, and that, without such ethical imperatives operating in the individual's mind, heart, and soul, a society cannot long endure and will soon enough sink into decadence and then collapse (Barzun 2000, Bloom 1994). Late Rome is the great example of that, and we are rapidly speeding in that same direction in today's "Runaway World" (Giddens 2002). In this manner, a primary stress on social utility paradoxically leads to the collapse of a society since it is not founded upon the ethically primary individual, who is the ultimate source of morality and thus social stability. Thus, right up front, I state that our examination of the moral will seek to probe the less examined domain of the inward—the subjective, that realm "where the meanings are," as Emily Dickinson put it.

To arrive at such a destination, one has many paths to choose from. Not one of them is free from what any life-path inevitably entails in this realm of existence: ecstatic ups and infernal downs; times in which the universe seems to be on your side and things go as smoothly as an azure ocean on a calm summer day, or when a tempest hits and every wave of life seems to be personally directed against you and you are on the verge of drowning to your horror and humiliation.

Some of the choices one is called upon to make are so emotionally stable and morally lucent that the decisions seem to just make themselves; other times, you will spend sleepless hours, your eyes turning to stone, as you turn a complex question over in your mind for the millionth time and are still no closer to resolution. One might describe the results of these encounters as either improving or degrading their character. The hope for many who find meaning in the moral domain, then, is that, through these encounters and by journey's end, each of their life's experiences will have brought them closer to their goal or destination.

In the end, what we need more than ever in these ethically problematic times we inhabit is a barometer of sorts, an instrument for those who seek information or even confirmation of intuition regarding the development of a person's character. For a message that spans the ages the ages, since at least the time of Plato and Aristotle, Seneca and Boethius, is the assumption that one's very human character can be as noble as the gods, as base as the underworld, and that man's journey as he comes into this world is filled with hope not only on what he shall make in the life, but also on what he shall become.

This is the difference between one's life being a narrative of suspicion and despair or one of faith and hope (Homans 1995, Ricoeur 1991). In the former kind of narrative, one's life is much more prone to spiral down into godless and grim worldviews, leading to even more self-destructive behavior. In the latter view, one's life is much more prone to spiral up into a sense of the Divine operating in one's life, which is all the inspiration one needs to lead an ever better life from year to year, month to month, day to day, even decision to decision. Which narrative do we want for our students? What narrative, indeed, do we want for ourselves? Clearly, it is the narrative of hope and belief. Without, of course, teaching this more spiritual view of life in inappropriate ways in the classroom, of course, let us lead our lives in such a manner, relate to our students in such a fashion, and write up or mange to teach existing curricula with the narrative of hope ever guiding as we and our students wrestle with the issues under analysis. Doing this, we will be teaching and our students will be learning in the Spirit. And the moral lesson that that kind of pedagogy will convey to our students will last them a lifetime, will abide perhaps even past this lifetime, and will make us teachers who, in the words of Malcolm Muggeridge, are devoted to doing "something beautiful for God."

THE STORY BEHIND THE TAXONOMY

I began this work over three decades ago (see chapter 3), during my years as a graduate student, looking for an acceptable dissertation topic. As a student studying under Kevin Ryan, Professor Emeritus at Boston University and Co-Founder of the Center for the Advancement of Ethics and Character, I had begun to read some of the literature. But while my readings waned, my own personal life waxed boldly. Indeed, anyone wanting to venture into this topic called "character education" ought to be warned up front that reading alone is not sufficient for true learning.

Ryan later wrote (*Building Character in Our Schools*, 1998) on the imperative of having to know the right, to feel the right, and to do the right. But, unlike most topics of inquiry, this would require much more than a knowledge of the material. Living through challenges in my personal life has been equally as important in the development of the taxonomy as have any books or articles on this subject matter. In fact, there were more than several occasions in the search for the best term required for a particular piece of the taxonomy where my own life's journey took me upon an important lesson— important enough to make clear and clean the very term I had been seeking. Serendipitous? Yes, at the least. Directed? Yes, at the best . . . and *this* is my belief. The funny thing is the more one allows oneself to believe in such direction in one's life, the more such direction manifests itself.

There is even a body of clinical evidence that this is so, starting with early experiments with people who exhibited certain special abilities—what are sometimes called "paranormal" gifts. Professor Rhine of Duke University found as early as the 1930's that the more that people believed that they possessed such talents, the more they were able to exhibit them in controlled experiments. What I am talking about here is much the same thing. Faith in divine direction leads to the appearance of such direction, and the more the faith, the greater the direction. We have it all turned around usually. Usually, people think, "Well, let some Higher Power show me its care for and guidance of me, and then I will put my trust in it." The reverse is generally the case, however. The more one trusts such a Higher Power, the more its hand becomes apparent in one's life. It is as if the Higher Power is waiting for us to step forth in faith and love before it begins to bestow its bounty upon us. And it does this not for Its own sake but for ours—so that we know that we have within ourselves the power and the passion to choose the higher vision and that we did not, in a smaller ethical fashion, wait until we had good old hard-and-fast evidence before we acted. No. That would simply be a bargain, a sort of "business deal" with the Divine. Rather, we were motivated by trust in higher truth, which indicates a noble character, not a cosmically "calculating" one.

As educators, none of this should not surprise us. For, do we not find that the more love and trust we invest in a class, the more it will respond to us? Maybe not the first day, the first week, or even the first month. But love and trust in higher truths is an eternal principle and a finally invincible power. As existential beings and also as pedagogical ones: "Faith precedes the miracle," as people of faith often advise us.

My own efforts in this field as a doctoral student would not be the way to go to write an acceptable dissertation (and by "acceptable" was clearly meant one that did not evidence any evidences of faith). For, I had prepared for it with abundant courses in methodology and a good deal of reading in philosophy. In spite of all this, I was learning that real scholarship entails being not only technically prepared but also spiritually prepared. Readers know when an author is writing from his own hard-won experience and when he is simply rambling on (however eloquently) about something that he himself has but scant personal experience of but knows only as a matter of theory.

At any rate, I was compelled to find a more manageable work to earn the degree, with hopes that eventually, I would return to the field of character education. Now, with less energy to bring to the screen, but with requisite experiences gleaned from a life far more focused, I returned to the doodles scratched upon airline napkins, the legal pads long put away many moves ago, geographical as well as psychospiritual, and what felt like as many moons ago, only ready in the last couple of years to surface yet again into new stacks of theorizing and positing practical directions to take in the classroom the piles of papers that lay like so many figures at Stonehenge on my desk.

It really began with my own interest in people's journeys, in theoretical model-building, having already been recruited by Kevin Ryan to co-author article with him focusing upon the developmental stages of a teaching career. Being a student and an ex-teacher of history (and now once again a high school teacher of United States history) had allowed me a certain leeway towards making generalizations surrounding world cultures. Becoming a professor, teaching both educational foundations and human development, has encouraged me to conjecture about patterns in the growth of a teacher, as well as the ideals worthy of serious reflection and effort. And finally, being a human being seeking to gain a true education exhorted me to go after the good (and, as Aristotle reminds us) not just the clever.

Light and darkness became the driving metaphor of the journey of the development of character, but only after the intensity and newness of the emotions which defined the experience began to wane. Certainly, the Gospel of John in the New Testament had its influence in my decision with his emphasis on light and darkness, and the light shining in the darkness and how the darkness could never finally overcome the light. And so, as I began to place a handful of ideals down on paper, haltingly as if they were those initial puzzle pieces that one begins to place on a card table ever so gently before giving oneself over the thousands of details, I began to realize that these ideals were the best thoughts of 4000 years of civilization. No matter the cynicism and relativism of our age, I began to see in these ancient writers the existence and guaranteed continuance of truths that come before us and go on long after us. They are simple ideas, but then again, all the best thinking and noblest actions come not from ever more subtle philosophical analysis but through firm and full ethical commitment to what is true and beautiful. It could not be simpler to understand, although putting it into action may prove to be the greatest challenge in one's life.

So *Truth* and *Beauty* became my first organizing principles. I felt those best (but not solely) presented by the Greeks as ideals worthy of striving for by any who would endeavor to live a life based upon the ideal rather than the carnal. *Obedience, charity,* and *faith* came next—again those best (but not solely) idealized by the other great peoples from the Mediterranean and the Desert: Moses, Jesus, and Mohammed. *Wisdom* came next. I felt it best represented in the best gifts from the Orient. *Joy* felt best as I thought about Africa—in all of my idealized understanding of that culture. *Virtue* also appeared in the doodles, undergirded by the study of the ancient peoples in Scandinavia. *Humility* came as well—most intuitive embodied for me in those I felt which were the best from the people of the Southern Americas. And then, in thinking about what peoples have most sought after in these parts, I took the ideal of *Liberty* from Northern America. And there, the ten ideals sat. Bill Fogt, my great colleague during our time teaching at BYU, scoured philosophy texts and read chunks of classical poetry. We dreamed of a significant work to be written. We became idealistic college students all over again. Even our teaching became noticeably more effective in the next couple of semesters. We talked much of our field of dreams, of walking into the cornfields and finding eternal beings, forever at play there. We presented these rudimentary sketches four, even five times within a year at regional and national conferences.

A silly idea, I thought, to dare and try my hand at suggesting what might be the aims of a character education. But, nonetheless, I overcame these inner deriding voices and let myself be drawn on by my better angels. And very slowly, one summer, the first attempts to find slightly less idealized terms, and then, their true opposites, started to take. It had not happened all at once—like Athena springing from Zeus' forehead. But this is the nature of creativity: It is generally slow, laborious, filed with missteps, stumbles and downright pratfalls. It is a very human thing—this thing we all call creativity. And like all birth, it entails blood, sweat and tears. This is why standardized education and mechanical assessment are absolutely inimical to creativity. If our goal is to douse any remaining sparks of creativity and godly potential in our children here in the increasingly confused and craven 21st century, then there is no better way to accomplish it than standardized education.

What emerged from my labors was the following: Ten columns, four terms per column. And with one research assistant interested in pursuing a rather imposing chunk of time with the Oxford English Dictionary, the synonyms began to materialize—the arguments to roll forth!

We stretched each of the ten columns to five shades. I quickly saw how the taxonomy could be stretched only slightly to be used for a new ratings system for the visual arts (something I hope to do in the near future). In fact, I quickly pasted together a scoring sheet and took it with me to look at first-run movies and score them far beyond the PG, PG-13 and R ratings that we are so familiar with today. Bill, who in addition to being a professor of education, was also a Colonel in the United States Air Force, quickly adapted it to use for a new leadership model. We even got to present our work to a group at the Pentagon. But, with its imperfections frustrating both of us, and a new school year at the university already starting up, we put it all away in the file drawer for another season—perhaps until after retirement!

In the meantime, I had become the happy recipient of a rather large white board, which was immediately hung in my office. I wrote all the terms neatly on the board in columns and then forgot about the board . . . until I began to notice a pattern. Once in a while a student would stop, stare, and ask with excitement, what was on the board. It turned out that these were the students who were to be connected to the work and would ask to be research assistants. And they proved to be great motivators, often inviting me to pick up the work yet again when I showed signs of slowing down or stopping.

Another year went by. My attention rested fully on a completely different issue within the field of Teacher Education—until a very patient research assistant had quietly constructed the taxonomy with six terms per column as well as two more columns. She was right on the mark. The entire circle (see below) fell into place. I was able to polish very quickly, by changing word orders and upgrading a few terms. *Honor and Sacrifice* became the final two ideals, terms not implicated by geography, but rather by all peoples who sought to be their best with their fellow man, and who gave of their offerings to their God. At the end of an entire decade (the 1990s) of formal, informal and even invisible investigation, it had come time to lay it out.

THE TAXONOMY FOR THE JOURNEY OF THE HEART

Describing the Taxonomy

How, then, might I begin my description of the journey through the varying shades of light and darkness? To understand what that goal or destination is, I have developed the taxonomy to gauge one's state or status *vis a viz* these ideals. The taxonomy, then, is a list of descriptor terms. At Level A, one finds the great ideas, of matters sublime, of the most exquisite qualities of character (any one of which has been almost universally agreed to). At Level F, one finds their antithesis. With the intermediate levels, one can find incremental steps between the two extremes.

Our goal in life is to perfect ourselves by gaining the purest of light or attributes—that is, the highest echelon within the taxonomies. When the higher attributes are obtained, we are as close as we can possibly come to the perfection we seek in this life in refining our own moral character. Though our goal is perfection, we will inevitably find ourselves at different points of light and darkness along the way. We all pass through different seasons of circumstances and distinct developmental periods. As we evaluate ourselves, we will find that we fall at different points in each of the columns of the taxonomy. During seasons of our lives, we may fall into the lower three rows of the taxonomy; at other times, we might strive to journey into the upper three rows. And most probably, if we take the moral journey seriously, we may find ourselves within years, and sometimes within days or even hours of both the upper and the lower rows in any column. This, I believe, is part of life and its refining fire.

But as time progresses, those who are guided by forces seen and unseen yet all of whom seek to take this moral journey find themselves more and more in the upper rows. As we gain greater light and knowledge through life experiences, we will take on the greatest of the attributes leaving us next to the divine impulses we wish to emulate. Of course, our own path is limited by the characteristics of the deity we choose to follow. This limitation falls beyond the scope of this work, but may be a fascinating derivative of this work for a comparative religion study.

Since the taxonomy is designed to allow one to evaluate his or her own character and identify areas of weakness and strength, then an interesting

Table 4.1: Light and Dark Aspects of the Moral Domain: Foundations of an Ethical Pedagogy

	Qualities Group 1	Qualities Group 2	Qualities Group 3	Qualities Group 4	Qualities Group 5	Qualities Group 6	Qualities Group 7	Qualities Group 8	Qualities Group 9	Qualities Group 10	Qualities Group 11	Qualities Group 12
L1	Truth	Beauty	Joy	Wisdom	Faith	Liberty	Virtue	Honor	Charity	Humility	Sacrifice	Immorality
L2	Knowledge	Esteem	Happiness	Understanding	Hope	Freedom	Integrity	Respect	Kindness	Meekness	Dedication	Life
L3	Realization	Admiration	Satisfaction	Learning	Desire	Right	Decency	Obedience	Passion	Deference	Contribution	Being
L4	Ignorance	Vanity	Pain	Disinterest	Doubt	Complacency	Corruption	Disregard	Indifference	Apathy	Waste	Silence
L5	Darkness	Malice	Misery	Deception	Fear	Despair	Immorality	Contempt	Lust	Pride	Greed	Death
L6	Blasphemy	Desecration	Agony	Hypocrisy	Horror	Bondage	Depravity	Abhorrence	Enmity	Arrogance	Mockery	Damnation

development can occur. Once those areas are identified, one may set goals to modify or improve upon one's character, allowing one to continually progress towards the perfected character one desires.

To be sure, perfection is a time-consuming process that spans far beyond a full lifetime. In my view, the desire for perfection is meant to encourage trajectory not just with the expectation of completion due to a lifetime of effort, but for becoming fully empowered as the creation that we are, with this mortal life being but a beginning, however meaningful and significant. Furthermore, and even more importantly, movements within a column are the normal course in mortality. For example, by examining column 9, one might choose to make the journey of the heart from passion to charity. But, that does not mean that lust would not be a temporary way station, let alone a test.

The taxonomy, as an instrument, also allows a user to analyze situations and events. As moments in time are analyzed, one will have a greater understanding of the character he/she possesses and manifests to others. This will again empower the person to make changes to drive towards perfections and a morally-based character. At that point, building character is a work more readily identifiable for discussions between student and teacher, parent and child, leader and adherent.

SUMMING UP

Locating the shades of light and darkness within each of us empowers us to reach our goals and aspirations. We may perfect our character and base it upon ideals of pure light or degrade our character and base it upon the realities of darkness. The taxonomy gives a tool to understand where we stand and in what direction we are heading. With its help, we can come ever closer—through the instrumentality of the curriculum that attends to these criteria—to the ethical ideal we seek. But, we must also be aware that while some are drawn to the light, others find themselves drawn to the powerful darkness that Levels D, E, and F represent. The taxonomy, thus, allows evil or darkness to be studied and understood.

To bring this chapter full circle, I note that to understand events such as those committed at Columbine High School and Tree of Life Synagogue is to reach into these lower levels. Certainly, we are not offering any explanation between what was felt and what was done: the work of the heart and the work of the hand. What we are suggesting is that for many of us it is inadequate and frustrating to limit the discussion of evil merely to a discussion of whether or not guns should be legal. Crimes committed, after all, are only crimes committed. In the first and most crucial place, it is the intentions of the heart that start the whole infernal process rolling. Let us look at such crimes in terms of their deep causes, not their surface-level manifestations and instrumentalities. That is no way to end the crime because it is not the way to understand the heart that instantiated the crime. It is when we make sense of the journey of the heart that we have the possibility of discovering what is playing out before us—and for educational processes to unfold in the service of the ethical fortifying of the student, the satisfaction of the teacher in his or her work, and a less fractious, more democratic society.

And, thus, in this day and age, with all its powerful arguments for reason above all, it may be wise once again to explore more seriously, to understand more seriously, the journey of the heart.

To help you do just that, following is a series of exercises that will help you examine yourself in a way that I hope you find enlightening and fun! I'll simply let this taxonomy speak for itself. Thus, I now offer the reader this summative theoretical model, including the *Ideals* that come from earlier chapters: Truth, Honor, Liberty, Beauty, Wisdom, Charity and Joy.

Working with the Journey's Taxonomy

Taking the taxonomy and organizing it into its six columns, notice the following headings:

Ideals	Virtues	Powers	Shadows	Failings	Poisons
Truth	Peace	Knowledge	Ignorance	Hostility	Blasphemy
Beauty	Kindness	Imagination	Isolation	Cruelty	Horror
Integrity	Harmony	Reason	Futility	Violence	Hypocrisy
Liberty	Organization	Obedience	Disregard	Rebellion	Agony
Love	Pleasure	Openness	Frustration	Pain	Torment
Joy	Happiness	Confidence	Uncertainty	Sadness	Grief
Humility	Sincerity	Vision	Delusion	Deception	Arrogance
Honor	Respect	Dignity	Defensiveness	Humiliation	Contempt
Faith	Clarity	Purpose	Emptiness	Confusion	Fear
Hope	Compassion	Passion	Vanity	Greed	Despair
Charity	Gratitude	Purpose	Withdrawal	Resentment	Enmity
Wisdom	Enlightened	Curiosity	Confusion	Darkness	Folly

Application #1: Self-evaluation:

Directions:

A. Choose one or two words where you have journeyed recently:

_____   _____

B. Choose one or two words where you would like to be shortly:

_____   _____

C. Study these terms—are they right? How do they make you feel?

_____

D. The take-away here: What can you now see about your journey?

_____

Application #2: Teacher evaluation:

A. Self-description
B. Student feedback
C. Can you identify what is holding you back from reaching the top tiers

Application #3: Curriculum development

A. What is the strongest identifiable term within your developed curriculum?
B. What is the weakest identifiable term?
C. What is the main purpose of securing terms for the affective domain in one's lesson?
D. Are there any lessons or sections that need revision to align with terms?

Application #4: New Video ratings system

A. What are the ranges identified by headings of the six columns that your YouTube clips invite students to feel?
B. Are ratings as they currently stand where they need to be?
C. Is there anything too intense for your audience, due to issues relating to maturity policies typically laid out for students under 18?
D. What type of letter to parents would you write to inform them of this taxonomy?

REFERENCES

Barzun, J. 2000. *From Dawn to Decadence: 500 Years of Western Cultural Life.* New York: HarperCollins.

Block, A. 1997. *I'm Only Bleeding: Education as the Practice of Social Violence against Children.* New York: Peter Lang.

Bloom, A. 1987. *The Closing of the American Mind.* New York: Simon and Schuster.

Homans, P. 1995. *Jung in Context: Modernity and the Making of a Psychology.* Chicago: University of Chicago Press.

Jung, C.G. 1954. *The Symbolic Life.* R. F. C. Hull, Trans. Princeton, New Jersey: Princeton University Press.

Kant, I. 1781/1997. *The Critique of Pure Reason.* Chicago: Hackett Publishing.

Mayes, C. 2020. *Archetype, Culture, and the Individual in Education: The Three Pedagogical Narratives.* Routledge: London.

Osguthorpe, R. 1995. *The Education the Heart.* Provo, Utah: Brigham Young University Press.

Otto, R. 1958. *The Idea of the Holy.* New York: Oxford University Press.

Ricoeur, P. (1991). *Freud and Philosophy: An Essay in Interpretation.* New Haven: Yale University Press.

Rogoff, B. *Apprenticeship in Thinking: Cognitive Development in Social Context.* New York: Oxford University Press, 1990.

Ryan, K. and K. Bohlin. 1998. *Building Character in Schools.* New York: Doubleday.

Chapter 5

Seven Pillars of Successful School Reform

Over twenty years ago, I had the privilege of presenting a paper at Aarhus Universitet, in Denmark, entitled "Journeys of the Heart: Uncovering the Roots of One's Morality." It had appeared to me during my doctoral dissertation years that the development of one's ethical system was much more significant than many educators and especially educational theorists were letting on.

By the 1980s and early 1990s, U.S. society had come far in expunging the imposition of certain privileged religious traditions in the public sector, whether in the public schools or in the surrounding society (Watras 2005). For me, this imposition, although not a practice that I advocate in a country where Jefferson's "Wall of Separation" between Church and State doctrine was of paramount importance, was totally understandable. In my experience, this was especially the case in a region where a particular religious tradition overwhelmingly dominates. I had personally witnessed this with teachers imposing their Catholic faith on students in Boston or their Mormon faith on students in Salt Lake City.

In one iteration of my proposal for a dissertation at Boston University, I wrote that for some of us deeply interested in the extracognitive of our field, education can be viewed as opening both the mind and the heart to moral dimensions. To truly educate is to guide a learner through what we call 'journeys of the heart,' finding selfhood, not just a greater range of intelligences.

In a later presentation, I introduced a taxonomy that attempted to clarify these gradations of curricula that ran through the mind, the heart, and the soul. This offered both the curricularist and the teacher a system which would: 1) allow them to investigate the structure (or, indeed, also the absence) of higher motivations in any given curriculum or approach to curriculum and 2) to create that reflected their own highest values and intentions. I intend to present that taxonomy in this chapter.

But before I do so, I will, as in previous chapters, reflect on my own personal experiences that underlay my formulation of this grand taxonomy. Almost ten years earlier, I had proposed a first chapter for my doctoral dissertation entitled "On What It Means to be a Morally Educated Person," which led my chair to pretty much have a cow. With one or two controversial citations, the 30-page effort was summarily dismissed and yours truly stepped away from scaling this final summit for a full year.

To be sure, Mormon life in Utah was slightly different from the intellectual life in Boston. But it reflected my deep desire to build one of my first bridges between the assumptions of the cognitive approaches to learning and the aspirations of the spiritual. Never did I want to impose my new religious belief on the one. Only that I would connect two of my core needs and gifts in this life. And if my heart ached for personal reasons, it was certainly torn on this bloody battlefield in a Boston University conference room (as my third reader so eloquently characterized it to me!).

I stated it this way: Over the course of the past ten years, both as a high school teacher and as a doctoral student, I silently, almost unknowingly gained a fascination for what educators call the 'null' curriculum; that is, the stuff that does not make it to the classroom, whether explicitly stated as part of the formal documents, generally thought to be the "curriculum," or implicitly as part of the style, the baggage that any teacher carries as part of himself or herself into the classroom. To be sure, there are several striking examples of this explicit or implicit curriculum for my perusal: the American history textbook that completely missed the point on what fueled Martin Luther King's mission; the controversial teacher who, unbeknownst to him/ her, verbally assaulted students with his/her firebrand of racist or sexist comments. These were easy. But what began as an uneasy sense of omission has blossomed into a raging fascination for this writer: that is, that part of an education that schools, even society, wishes to ignore, whether out of ignorance or, as Christian Fundamentalists claim, out of conspiracy.

Continuing on, I recalled my first day in the doctoral program. The quotation that Professor Ryan laid out before us, taken from Aristotle of course, was this: "The point of an education is not only to make the student smart but also to make him good." which registered with about as much delicacy as a thunderbolt in the desert. Indeed, not just the fact that I had grown up in suburban New York City, but even more recently, I had had the good fortune of teaching a whole bunch of very bright students in the suburbs of Miami for five years. Some had gone on to some of the country's very selective college and universities. But a gnawing feeling wouldn't go away—if they are so smart, why were more than a few of them in so much trouble with their personal lives?

It had come time to address this matter, to explore the world of the moral fabric, not just the intellectual paper. And so, during the classroom years of graduate study, I often searched for ways in which to express these concerns to laypeople, either through illustration, through parable, or through the ubiquitous backs of napkins. I began to make use of oversimplified models so that I could quickly sketch them out. These visual aids became useful in presenting and in organizing this genre of idea to friends and family alike. Their use also forced me to make good sense, lest I fall into the snare of the sweet but babbling doctoral student. And so, on the napkin, the intellect went left, the sentiment went right; and if the spiritual was up top, then the physical was at bottom. Four squares arranged in a diamond pattern, with the connection of the spiritual and the physical being defined as the soul.

Easy peasy as they say these days in these parts. But, not a universal. Not even amongst adult educators I have met along the way, especially in big cities. One of my first realizations was that while everyone was quick to realize the importance of being moral, no one could suggest where this quality resided. If "smarts" was a matter for the intellect, was morality a matter-or the emotional? Certainly it could not reside within the body (as anything carnal seemed to smack of immorality); so, then, was it to be found in the spiritual? But, then, weren't we getting much too close to that great trap of straying into the world of religion?

George Washington, in his Farewell Address if 1796, called religion and morality "the indispensable supports of political prosperity." He doubted that morality could be maintained without religion and suggested that these two are "the great pillars of public happiness and the firmest props of the duties of men and citizens" (Bellah 1996, 222). And so, I began in those formative years, allowing myself to venture anywhere matters of significance was to be found. There were to be no "out of bounds" for this study—if I needed to read from the great secular minds, so be it; but, if I needed to inspect or even borrow from writers with a religious bent, then that would be fair game as well.

A funny thing happened to this country on the way to establishing itself as one of the great powers in the history of the world. It has to do with a loss of surety of what we value, and of what Nietzsche called "a shared sense of the sacred," which is the surest way to recognize a culture and the key to understanding it and all of its facets (Bloom 1987, 204).

PILLAR #1: ON SUSTAINABILITY AND EDUCATION

For the past 140 years, America's public school system has been utilizing its most important resource—teachers—at a ghastly rate of mental/emotional/spiritual energy consumption. This rapid consumption of human capital (as evidenced by a 40%–60% "burn (out) rate every five or so years) reveals little evidence of acceptable sustainability." Today, there are districts that scrounge for scores of teachers with just days to spare before the opening of a new school year. School districts in Las Vegas, Los Angeles and New York City have each been written about extensively. In Utah and Salt Lake Counties, I (as a college supervisor for teacher candidates) witnessed classrooms with 35 and even 40 students, class sizes that I understand have gotten even bigger in recent years. Highly experienced master teachers are telling me that "warehousing" is now how they see their work, as they find precious little opportunity to offer effective instruction. Sustainability, in this case, has been maintained while the profession as a craft, has been sacrificed.

But, while, at the state level, hundreds of millions of dollars are spent to build new schools, there is something even more pernicious that is occurring long before the reported outcomes. For, if sustainability is up for grabs at the operations level it is more the case that sustainability becomes elusive at the conceptual level first.

"No Child Left Behind" was promulgated as a panacea to create universally-high standardized curricula and instruction in the United States. It's primary tool was high-stakes testing to determine which child should be directed towards which slot to occupy so that he will be an uncritical worker in a total state. If it seems alarmist to sound this trumpet, recall that the greatest of all U.S. educational historians, Lawrence Cremin (1988), warned over three decades ago that the primary threat to American democracy had become the growth of the military-industrial-*educational* complex. The educational goal of this "complex" would be to create students who would fit into the new total corporate state that keeps some of the superficial trappings of democracy but that is governed by covert elites.

John Dewey would raise cries to high heaven about any school in a democracy that does not dedicate itself to speaking truth to power instead of simply conforming to it, which is, of course, precisely the purpose of standardization. Such a view of producing quality products might work on an assembly line— although even here it is questionable. What makes it problematic, even tragic, when applied to education is that students are not products on an assembly, or at least should not be!

I think it has come time to take a closer look at the connection between environmental sustainability and school teacher sustainability, for I believe that deficits in both tell us quite a bit about the American approach to "sustainers"—that is to say, to those who nurture or sustain our society. If we can surmise the more fundamental elements in these two stories—say, conquest through arrogance in the former and abandonment through ignorance in the latter—we would be better able to detail a reality worthy of serious consideration and constructive critique. In the end, without such a perspective, sowing and reaping on the land could be misunderstood for slashing and raping of the land. And in education, investment tied to a one-size-fits-all performance schedule might easily turn into an Orwellian brave new millennium.

To establish the parallelism between the land and teachers, I shall begin with an examination of the former. Two ideas come to mind regarding our relationship with the land. Most of us who grew up in this country are well aware of the notion of Manifest Destiny: the challenging idea that the American continent was seen as "ripe for the picking." For those not raised here, this was a term coined in this country in the 1840's, quickly marshaled as the justification for Anglo habitation and then domination from the Atlantic to the Pacific. Succeeding generations would be forced to face three possible interpretations here.

Anglo occupiers had done not with the land but to the land. What this habitation and then domination of the land actually meant logistically ethically was three-fold: first, it demonstrated that we were unable to view the land as an object worthy of our care; second, it underlined our inability to view the land as an object worthy of our care, indeed as something we were ethically bound to protect, not ravage; and third, it showed up in a star light our callous view of the land as something to be wantonly taken advantage of because it was so bountiful that we would never face any consequences for cravenly drawing from her with no regard for her limits.

These types of realities were assumed until our own generation. Only with our generation have these grim implications become clear to us so that we have tried to compensate for our dreadful past relationship to the land with more enlightened views and nurturing agricultural practices. And is it not possible that, in the collective cultural consciousness of Anglo America, we chose to physically liberate the Africans we had grabbed as a tool of production only to replace that sin with another subjugation: the physical incarceration and torture of the land upon which we lived.

Environmentalism probably began in earnest in this country with Rachel Carson's *Silent Spring*, written in 1962. Fortunately, it would take only one generation to notice, with protests being carried out over corporate and individual selfishness resulting in toxic waste, our addiction relating to fossil fuel use, and our arrogant indifference related to global warming.

Condescension over a race of people may seem hard to understand for our current generation, but condescension for our Earth and all its offerings to us humans remains hard to change in our generation. We treat someone in an inferior manner when we completely fail to see his or her lack of value *apart* from their own utility *for us*. We also treat the Earth—its air, water, soil—in an inferior manner when we fail to see its value *apart* from its own utility *for us*. It appears that the arrogance of possession begot marginalization. Marginalization opened the door to a relationship based upon violence.

This established a vertical relationship of dominance with the land—an environmental hegemony that is finalized by emotional abandonment. The goal, at once hardheadedly practical and enormously idealistic, of reining in our lifestyle in order to achieve sustainability became irrelevant, if not laughable, because impossible in light of people's intransigent practices of "conspicuous consumption."

The idea of "conspicuous consumption" comes from the sociologist Thorstein Veblen in his 1899 classic in economics, *The Theory of the Leisure Class*. He argued that capitalist societies, because they value objects and consumption above all things, easily fall into patterns of people buying and consuming objects well beyond their needs to show others how "virtuous" and "powerful" they are in not only fulfilling the capitalist imperative to consume but are taking it to ever higher levels by consuming in excess.

For those of us in the field of education, the story is similar, although not identical. School, in America, was meant as a place to prepare for life. In some generations such as ours, the emphasis was on the wants of capitalism—the economic side of life; in other generations, it was based upon the needs of democracy—the social side of life; in one or two, it focused upon the desires of the individual—the psychological dimension. John Dewey wrote a whole lot about the needs of democracy and education's role, but he is most remembered as one who saw school not as a preparation for life but as life itself.

The problem of sustainability in education lies not at the amount of money spent or not spent (although such expenditures may tell us a lot about what we *really* want for and from educators.) Sustainability is attainable, once again, when there is recognized value in the enterprise apart from the investor's needs. Why would the investor (or here, the state) find value in teachers—although they are every bit as important to the survival of this nation as a democracy as the great forests and deserts and swamplands are? First, there is the problem of teachers being disconnected to the adult world—their clientele, even the rhythm of their days and their year tied in to the rhythms of children and adolescents. For urban Americans, school was not as tough as the adult's workplace, and thus teachers were not considered worthy of investment. For rural Americans, school was possibly a sideshow from the exigencies of daily life; thus, teachers were not deemed worthy of respect. Sustainability falls short because of the assumptions built into these relations.

Second, there was this "small" issue of the school being women's work, which has, until this past decade, held for at least for elementary education. In the 19th century, school-teaching was only a stopping off point for women to earn enough for a dowry and then to move on into marriage (Goldstein 2014). Today's students continue to be haunted with the notion that their work is temporary—individuals going into teaching to put the spouse through graduate school, only to leave the profession as soon as mission is accomplished, is a very common pattern among our academic-minded. Sustainability is not only elusive, but not reasonable to demand.

Third, there exists the notion that school is really a throwback to a sort of pastoral ideal, a time before the Industrial Revolution, when what mattered most were personal, familial, ethnic and subcultural ties. In sociology, this arrangement of one's life around local concerns is called Gemeinschaft—generally translated as "community" in English. Coined by the sociologist Ferdinand Tönnies in 1889, *Gemeinschaft* is a term connected to the person, to the family, to the tribe. This means that for most Americans, school is decreasingly relevant to the concerns of the "truly modern" person. It is a throwback to grandpa's day. Thus, it is not worth placing in such old-fashioned things as public schools the energy and resources that we would be better directed to matters and institutions that have to do with the larger-scale, more stressful demands of *Gesellschaft*—or "society"—the intellectual, the systemic, the institutional, the corporate, wrote, the really significant because in the present. The more impressive sounding *Gesellschaft* is increasingly and dramatically privileged in terms of funding and general public attention than are matters of *Gemeinschaft*.

Teaching, like the land herself, speaks volumes about connections for the purpose of relationship. The existence of workers in the industrial or even postindustrial world spoke volumes about connections for the purpose of individual gain. Sustainability became collateral damage for teachers as well as for the land; capital would fuel sustainability for the modernists.

In the end, to reward teachers to a level of sustainability is to recognize the value they contribute to the capitalist world. One would think that this is a straightforward and obvious thing to request of citizenry. But apparently, for many, the stretch is simply too great to accord teachers any special recognition for the positive effect that they have. Kids are not yet the adults required for capitalism; furthermore, for many of the parents, there is a deep ambivalence as to whether such a development towards adulthood would be desirable. I believe this to be counterfactual. Prominent educational historians like Rury (1989), Cuban (1993), and Vinovskis (1985) made it clear some time ago that, although teachers have never been paid exorbitantly, (or even particularly well), they tended to be public figures of substance, to whom people listened, especially in politics official and unofficial.

Again, two issues can shed light. First, there is the notion of how to measure inputs. For most businessmen and women, the input is measured by the number of hours spent. For teachers, I would like to propose that a better measure is the number of kilocalories expended. Second, there is the problem of filters. For most businessmen and women, filtering (as in secretaries screening phone calls) or sequencing (as in voicemail or e-mail that is taken one at a time) is assumed. For teachers, the lack of filtering is assumed (no secretaries, no phones, no sequencing to others' demands).

In this case, we treat someone in an inferior manner when we completely fail to see the degree of difficulty of their work. We utilize a measure of input that does not answer to the reality of their efforts, their value and their worthiness of sustainability. We talk to and about teachers out of a vast ignorance of what it is that they do, how much they accomplish (often against almost impossible odds), and how deeply they care about this country and its young people and fervently wish to guarantee the future of both. This ignorance begets marginalization. Marginalization, in this case, begets the offering of crumbs for remuneration. Our vertical relationship with the teacher is assuaged by pity. Sustainability becomes secondary if not a foreign idea. Hence, half of America's teaching force disappears every five years, and these are some of the major reasons why.

If we choose to look closely at our mean-spiritedness regarding Mother Earth, we also find a similar mean-spiritedness for the shepherds of our youth and our adolescents. Both embody an assault upon that which we foolishly believe cannot fight back. Both evidence an arrogance on the part of the male warrior-type, who see land as a something for the take, who see teachers not to be taken seriously. This is especially true at the elementary level because these "warriors" put teachers on a par with their wives, whom they see as "second-class citizens." To men in the schools, the warriors also accord only a contingent valuation. The warrior sees the public school male men typically at the secondary level, because they are in no way at par with themselves. In the warrior's eyes, the teacher's work is quaint, but never physically exhausting. Their efforts are laudable, but never commensurate. Their very being is pleasant but never understood.

The land, symbol of the mother throughout history since both bring forth life and sustain it, can be raped. The teacher can be dismissed. To sustain either one would require nothing less than a monumental shift in America's obsession with the warrior's outlook. For the land, like the woman, calls for respect in a host of other ways that call for kindness, empathy, reverence, and subtle service—none of which is a feature of economic or military conquest. "No dumping allowed" would have to be extended from the physical landscape to the emotional landscape. For the teacher calls for respect.

It has come time to call forth a new relationship between humankind and the land. And it has come time to call forth a new relationship between men and teachers. My hope is that the recent past, with the COVID-19 pandemic, has opened the eyes of millions of American parents to the work of teachers, now understood as hardly not as easy as "summers off," but perhaps simply as major league professionals who have earned an "off season."

In the end, we are in danger of coming to an age when hardware will *triumph* over Mother Earth, thus fulfilling the fear of the present youth. And even more disturbing, we are in danger of coming to a time when software will *replace* humanity, thus confirming the fear of many of today's teachers. Artificial intelligence may yet lead us towards a brave new world. But, before that year comes, it must be made clear what such a heartless triumph would entail, what psychosocial ills it would cause to rain down upon our heads in toxic world-historical storms when technology, not the individual with her complex individual personal and social needs, was in charge of social planning and its execution. The notion of sustainability has not only arrived in time, it may very well have come just in time.

PILLAR # 2: HOW WE AS EDUCATORS NEED TO RETURN AND NOURISH OUR ROOTS IN ORDER TO HELP OTHERS.

Roots

For those of us in our older-adult years, that TV miniseries in the late 1970s offered much to learn, much to talk about. Indeed, it left a powerful mark in our lives. Roots, for the younger adult generation. Roots, for most of us, imply where our grandparents raised our parents.

I wish to take this simple word and, like bread dough, knead it over and over until we find that it rises into a loaf that is studded with the fruity morsels of stories and possibilities. One thing I do know as an educator: part of me wishes to make it simple and connect to the kid within (child's play) but part of me wishes to discover complexity and engage with the adult without (grown-up play).

And what better than a story to satisfy both the need for play and the desire for complex insights? Hence, four stories, each entitled "Root," follow.

Four Stories

"Roots," as in the source of a toothache. "Yikes, I want to know where *this* pain comes from." Nourishing these roots would be about the urgency of digging and uncovering for the purpose of alleviating one's present pain—to ameliorate the problem at its foundation. Cleaning, drilling, filling, reconstructing are all attempts to strengthen foundations. For the purpose of the teacher and the writer (and almost every professor is by definition a writer) sometimes it is necessary to take a look at one's training, one's passions, one's purposes once again. A training may have rotted, a passion may have decayed, a purpose may have shifted. And so, returning to one's roots may be unsettling at best, if not downright unnerving (sorry!) but terribly important for the further well-being of each of us. For example, although I earned a doctorate in education, I have come to find certain flaws in its composition. And so, I will have to do some restoration in the near future if I want my advanced degree to support future work—just as restorative work at the root level is meant to do that for teeth. I call this sense of roots *understanding*.

"Roots," as in the spirit of understanding which impels some individuals to conduct family history searches. "Yes, I want to know where I come from." Nourishing these roots would justify the labor of digging for and uncovering information about the past, for such information is crucial for the purpose of shedding light upon one's present worldviews and attitudes. Thus, we can find that returning is to discover poorly understood links to those who have gone before us, and that nourishing is the attempt to do something to strengthen that story. Remembering, honoring, and for many in Utah, baptizing are all ways to claim roots for the purpose of strengthening our being. In my case, teaching is to make connections so that story becomes endowed with perspective, imbued with meaning, enlightened with other's completed lives. I call this sense of roots *connection*.

Roots, as in where one might seek clues about one's own personal journey. Driving past a house in which one spent considerable time as a child is a Pestalozzian object lesson that often teaches us far beyond the old pictures or videos. For it invites images, emotions, conclusions left unfinished, turns that one took along life's road, sometimes in a twinkling of an eye. For the teacher, returning to one's roots can cause a revisiting with all relationships, those who tutored us and the origins of our sense of calling as teachers. Nourishing one's roots with this approach celebrates life, which can only inform and inspire. The personal is drawn out, providing color for the black and white world of the professional. I call this sense of roots *clarity*.

Roots, as in "when the sun was up, (the seeds) were scorched; and because they had no root, they withered away." This reference, as written in the Book of Matthew among other gospel accounts, points to the story of how the search for one's roots is to gain fullness in growth. The fullness, of course, is not in a type of self-advertising, coy and vain, peacock-feather variety. It is in growth that reaches down, not out, a connection that seeks origin, not just destination. Sometimes it is necessary to take a look at one's education, one's voice once again. An education may need updating, one's voice may even have become timid, cynical, weary, or bland. And so, returning to one's roots as a writer may be difficult at best, if not downright depressing. But it is a positive depression that results in creativity. Jung said that depression often precedes creative acts because it is one's unconscious gathering energy to itself and mulling over a problem for which an answer is about to burst forth in the creative act. So let us not disparage our depressions too much. Rather, let us use them to be more fruitful in our work as a time of deep self-reflection just before the sunrise of creativity. I call this one *balance*.

Review

First, let's review for understanding. We return to roots because, like a toothache, there might be something painful that makes it worth taking the time and energy to address. It is to reveal impediments.

Second, for connection. We return to roots because, like family searches, there might be a part of a story missing that makes it worth taking the time and spending the energy to understand better. It creates new possibilities.

Third, for clarity. We return to roots, because one's own workalike may need focus, enough that makes it worth taking the time and spending the energy to see how far and in what direction we have journeyed. It is to secure vision.

Fourth, for balance. We return to roots, because, like a tree in a vineyard, there might be the need to ensure sources of strength, to secure healthy inputs not just outgrowths. It is to offer choice.

Whatever your work, with any or all of these, you have just examined, tended to, honored and increased what it is that you have to offer.

Teachers, Writers and Tutors: Just for You

For the teacher, the story may be burnout; it may be a need to deepen his/her understanding of the subject matter; it may be a story of how lasting the commitment in order to determine whether or not to continue with the work as a now-potential career; or it may be a celebration with how much one has truly accomplished.

For the writer, it may bring forth a difficult piece, for birthing, as it were, a very large "baby"; it may be to make important connections to styles of other writers; it may be the need to "get real" with one's ability; or it may be for the purpose of celebrating how mature one's writing has become.

For the tutor, it may be to revisit why we desire to work with people in the first place, how we work hard at connecting with each other; or then again, it may be to celebrate our desire to assist, even empower the other.

Personal Practice

The teacher. As a teacher, I have recently felt called to "return to my roots" because I have been experiencing considerable emotional and physical pain. The good news about pain is that the learning curve is fantastically steep.

There is no hemming or hawing about what is really going on. Once one gets past the primal panic reflex, one finds that pain is very wise, an organic alert to a person that something is very wrong physically or emotionally and that the time to deal with it is now. Uncovering the roots of my sense of calling as a teacher, I find that I have come to see that I teach because I want to share my passion with others. I have come to understand that passion also has a downside. The heart, when engaged, becomes vulnerable. Precision may be lost in translation. Further confusing pedagogical self-reflectivity is other external factors. For example, subject matter has gone through several revisions. Technology, always, has been upgraded. But to sort through all of these factors, internal and external, was worth it in the long run because it yielded truth, which must ever be the aim of all our inquiries.

The writer. As a writer, I am being called to "nourish"' my ideas by getting serious about writing. The work that I must own is why we must hold onto and embed philosophical ideals in the preparation of the next generation. *Ideals like wisdom, honor, beauty, integrity, charity, joy.*

The tutor. While I'm not typically a tutor, I find myself more and more being referred to as mentor. What I have learned from students recently is that they are ready and willing for me to learn from them. To encourage them to believe that I am earnest in this desire, I make sure that I allow the student various opportunities to step forward and express their own opinions, not just mimic (what they think are) mine. I let them know, both through explicit and implicit messages, that I do not play the game that we all know so well, for we have all been students in at least a few classes where the iron dictate is: "I am the teacher-god who knows everything; you are the servant-student whose only role is to take in what I say and repeat it back to me on tests."

I let them level the classical classroom setup: "I get to give, you get to receive." Returning to my roots by reflecting on myself as a teacher has allowed me to be successful in creating classrooms that challenge the comfort zones of traditional lines of relationship there. For, comfort zones, no matter the degree of academic separation between student and teacher, must be challenged if authentic I–Thou relationships are to prevail in the classroom. This does not mean that the teacher's degrees mean nothing. They are of great value. Nor does it mean the teacher becomes a "buddy" to his students. His authority is well-deserved. Only, he must refer to the degrees and wear his authority lightly, in a way that invites students into the possibility of learning from but also growing with him at the same time.

Your Turn

Finally, it's time for you to focus upon your stay or your return. For some of you will have the need to return because the lessons from pain, connection, clarity and balance await you. Some of you will have the need to return because the mystery is calling you. Some because the replanting is calling you. Some because your life's journey is calling you.

Nourishing our roots in order to help others is not the same as simply strengthening our own efforts. Our work is not only to do more of the same. It is to grow or mature what it is we have to offer, to make what we teach more powerful, to offer what we write with greater insight, to share how we tutor/mentor as more personal.

Nourishing these roots offers ourselves a continuing education, a greater delight in our own maturation and development. We find that we can truly help others not because of our success, but because we are able to flesh out human existence, not with sharper methods and techniques, but with more significant meaning and relationship. And so, after your work has served you well because you have served it well, remember that serving must not just carry on, but must also call forth. You. And your journey. Back to your roots. So that others' branches can be supported throughout all your days and all their yearnings.

PILLAR #3: THE WORK OF A TEACHER

If the work of a teacher is first to "lay out" and then "move out" with a curriculum, there is a secondary and a third work that comes almost simultaneously. The second work is to present the student with reasons to achieve; the third work is to find the right moment to tap into adolescent dreams. Let me explain.

One of the poorly understood aspects of an outstanding teacher is that he or she must do more than motivate the adolescent to perform. While this is the hallmark of achievement that our current-day tests are so hungry to measure, it misses the other half of the equation. Adolescents obviously stand halfway between youth and young adulthood. Their lives are not only fraught with intensity, but are really balancing acts between the need for mental development and the hunger for emotional passion. In other words, there is a need for both head and heart, much to the chagrin of school administrators who have their hands full with the communities, small to large, we have built in the name of sports-powered high schools.

Simmeringly, volatile at best, explosive any worst, these factories have the dubious distinction of having to control the inmates at every turn of the hallway. From double periods introduced to halve the number of "passing times" in the hallways to lunch periods extending across most of the midday (to spread out the mayhem so that it might actually settle down enough to turn into a proper meal and some "chill time"); from marks of achievement warped by school attendance/tardy policies to medicines controversial enough to question the entire system's legitimacy; to the large high schools we have chosen to build since 1950 (even with our new countermodels of small schools and charter schools) that are architected and raised in the name and glorification of efficiency. And with efficiency for the capitalist tool, we find ourselves making the heart extinct, save it be for the passions of the playing field.

But if the passion of a great lesson has become rare, if the ability of the master teacher to teach something far beyond the facts du jour is threatening, if the ability of the system to *trust* these extraordinary mentors and advisers is frightening, there is also the problem that *what* we have decided to teach remains lodged somewhere in the mid-20th century: English, Social Studies, Math, Science, Foreign Languages, and Elective. Furthermore, we have demanded that others be trained only in such narrow subject matters. What we have chosen to teach continues to serve the university, which continues to serve the notion that a specialized body of knowledge is the only way to know anything.

I suspect that the introduction of the International Baccalaureate program began to break the hold of these assumptions, and that really progressive charter schools also broke the mold of such assumptions as well. But, lurking deeper than these progressive outcroppings is the question for higher education to try and make sense of it all in the first place. And now, since higher education's delivery system as well as its curricular offerings are in serious (and probably historically shattering) debate, then the high school's curricular assumptions are next.

Education without a Soul

Early in the 20th century, the British poet T.S. Eliot lamented: "Where is the wisdom we have lost in knowledge? Where is the knowledge we have lost in information?" (1971, 201) That cry is still relevant today, perhaps even more so. The wisdom of general truths that reflect the perennial realities of the human condition have been dismissed by postmodern philosophy on the brash assumption that there are no general truths available to human-kind—that there is nothing reliable enough that might light us a path forward through the dark forest of this life. This leaves us ethically desolate, stranded, and starving for moral sustenance. That is the wisdom we have lost in merely theoretical knowledge, says Eliot. But it gets even worse. For that knowledge itself soon is made secondary to its mere instrumental uses, its "information" value. Against this counterintuitive and destructive notion, I assert that it is the universal that must be available, not to counterbalance the particular, but rather to undergird our understanding and uses of the particulars of our seventh millennial world. Education, then, must consider the return to the deeper ethical meaning, and not to just the rush to the latest factual discovery. For, "where there is no vision, the people perish" (Proverbs 29: 18)

What does this mean for the teacher? It means that knowledge, understanding and wisdom are his and her goals, some attainable in the short run, some approachable in the longer run. It means that the struggles for offering such knowledge, for demanding the mastery of such knowledge, must just be a part of the process. Students must also learn how such knowledge is arrived at—through making connections far deeper than E.D. Hirsch's mere mastery of various "packages" of knowledge. And it means that the master teacher must not only teach with head and heart, but, as Harvard professor Gere Murphy suggested years ago, that he and she must lead with soul. What matters most in deep and true educational processes is to reveal the struggles of those who have given us the wisdom that I am calling for and that students are in desperate need of. It is to revel in the surprises. It is to refute the easy answers. It is to renounce the road of accomplishment only.

Head, heart and soul point to one thing in particular, It is towards the purpose of inspiring the student, so that in his and her aspirations, *dreams* are once again accepted. For, there are dreams of adolescence that must be identified; they must be guarded; they must be clearly delineated as "hallowed ground." For those dreams provide the best energy source the student will find for their long-term battery, giving them fuel far beyond the cheap octane booster of just "getting good grades." This is the high calling and unique task, then, of teacher: to bring together the needed achievement with the hoped-for dreams for a truly dynamic education. What prods the dreams, what kindling wood might be found for such a roaring fire, will be revealed just a bit farther along.

PILLAR #4: JOURNEYS OF THE HEART

Uncovering the roots of the student's morality. For some of us deeply interested in the extracognitive of our field, education can be viewed as opening both the mind and the heart to moral dimensions. To truly educate is to guide a learner through what we call "journeys of the heart," finding selfhood, not just a greater range of intelligences. This presentation will introduce a taxonomy through the use of analytic philosophy. Understanding the "shades of light" embedded in this complex taxonomy will then allow the learner-investigator to discern his or her intentions, even motivation, in learning.

In seeking to connect theory to practice, the taxonomy is then activated by coupling verbs with nouns. These activated pairs of terms are then molded into concentric circles, enabling the story of a personalized journey to unfold.

By investigating the entire self, each individual will be able to acquire a more complete education, and thus access a greater range of intelligences.

Applying this unified field theory to schooling and to education as a whole, I venture in a different direction from the hoped-for panacea of the silicon chip (Goldstein 2014). Since I seek to build a stronger curriculum and to identify more effective instruction, some might label my work as back-to-basics. I describe my work as back-to-the-core. What must occur is a reconnection of both formal curriculum and instruction to the affective domain. With this stereophonic capacity (the cognitive *and* the affective), teachers become more capable guides for their assigned learners.

However, before any serious applications are entertained, educators must first understand and apply this type of instruction to themselves as they are invited to engage in a process that can lead to enhanced self-realization. Then we can, and will, explain how the taxonomy is linked formally to academic subjects. And additional application involves its use as an evaluation tool for techs. And, by reformatting the taxonomy into a student self-evaluation students will find themselves better equipped to identify both their heartfelt intentions and their desired destinations. Such results will assist guidance counselors, parents, and teachers seeking to obtain a more in-depth picture of the student's deepest intentions, which will, in turn, offer a basis for designing the broadest and most relevant education.

Such applications empower educators to promote the discovery of "self" and to discover the fullness of intelligences among learners. This journey of the heart is a critical aspect in securing a complete education. For when intentions of the heart and destinations of one's desires intersect, intelligences are activated and selfhood is realized. Education then not only provides knowledge and understanding, but also uncovers the roots of one's morality. This offers all parties a more complete picture of an education now worth its weight in gold, as intentions are clearly understood as fundamental complements to what is going on in the minds of the student. And perhaps even of the teacher!

This is a truth that, although not spoken of very much in educational "research," is the very heart and soul of much great literature. Chaim Potok wrote in *The Chosen,* "A heart I need for a son. A soul I need for a son, compassion I want from my son, righteousness, mercy, strength to suffer and carry pain, that I want from my son, not a mind without a soul!" And in his delightful classic *The Little Prince,* Antoine de Saint-Exupery (2001, 34) wrote, "Now here is my secret, a very simple secret: It is only with the heart that one can see rightly, what is essential is invisible to the eye."

PILLAR #5: A CLOSER EXAMINATION
OF THE JOURNEY'S IDEALS

The three domains revisited. Throughout this study, I have referred to the three basic domains that Bloom defined as crucial for the educator to know about and to operate with ease within. It has proven immensely popular over the decades. I'll give it again here for the reader's convenience:

1: The cognitive domain. This is the domain on which schools typically focus—excessively so, in fact, to the exclusion of all else that concerns or comprises the child. Its importance cannot be denied, nor would I ever wish to do so. My objection is to its almost total control of the ethos and curricula of the school. It includes knowledge, respect, freedom reason, obedience, curiosity, purpose. This is what schools think about and what is a first line for education.

2 and 3. The affective and the spiritual domains, respectively, cry out for other elements of experience and other species of knowledge, such as sincerity, admiration, desire, esteem, understanding, and passion, as well as conviction, compassion, choice, connection, devotion, and stillness. It is these that make up "the journey of the heart," and it is precisely these that find but little attention in the school's agenda.

The Six Ideals

When the ideals for a complete education come together, regardless of culture and of century, the three domains—the cognitive, the affective and the spiritual—also come together as a complete set of intelligences. It is at this point that those educational ideals that were held and promulgated by the great philosophers and educators come within our reach. As I have come to parse those ideals over many years of formulating them for pedagogical purposes, they are:

1. Truth and beauty
2. Liberty and honor
3. Wisdom and charity

If we place these ideals in a vertical column, we find the following ingredients able to inform, strengthen and capture these ideals. Thus,

Truth	Knowledge, Sincerity, Conviction
Beauty	Respect, Admiration, Compassion
Liberty	Desire, Choice, Freedom
Honor	Devotion, Obedience, Esteem
Wisdom	Curiosity, Connection, Understanding
Charity	Stillness, Passion, Purpose

What occurs now is that the curricula have become rounded and rejuvenated. Some of these terms are the works of the mind; others are the longings of the heart; and still others point to the stirrings of the soul. Those that point to the mind involve Justice (the Letter of the Law); those that point to the heart involve Mercy (the Spirit of the Law); and, those that remain apart point to righteousness (The Intent of the Law). By putting these all together, putting them all in alignment, we wind up with something exciting—a 7th ideal. It is *Joy*—the human being's highest aspiration.

PILLAR # 6: CONNECTING THE IDEALS TO THE CURRICULUM

In order to restore the classic core curriculum (Science, Technology, Engineering, Arts [yes, some of you forgot!]), and Mathematics, we need to look closely at what we want schools to offer. For, without a carefully examined foundation of education, the students will pick up on its disconnectedness, if not its irrelevance to their lives. Indeed, our curriculum is horribly disconnected to early 21st-century life. And so, here are some questions from the various disciplines that I propose to jumpstart our thinking. They are not the only questions we might ask by any means. They are simply representative of the kinds of questions we should be asking in education.

1. What does U.S. history have to say about those who hate us?
2. What does American literature tell us about America?
3. How can math empower soon-to-be consumers?
4. Is there another way of knowing beyond the scientific method for right-brained students?
5. Are music, art, theater and PE offering anything of substance or of value to this generation of students?
6. Why can't we make up our minds for once and for all to teach English *and* Spanish to all of our students? And if not, why not put students with little or no English speaking/writing abilities into an intensive language course, the way that Latter Day Saints who go on their church missions, spend 8 weeks in intensive training and then head out to their

assignment? Because I'd settle for a full semester (16 weeks) for most, and even a full year (32 weeks) for those who need more time. After all, what is the problem with graduating high school at 19 rather than at 18?

The needs of society and the child can be laid out as follows:

1. We always need more economic skills. These will never stop being highly desirable in the global economy.
2. We are also in need of greater civic skills. These will never stop being highly important in our democracy, or whatever is left of it to repair!
3. We need to be an informed and an enlightened citizenry, just as Thomas Jefferson insisted. Schools must address this *dual* need of American society: tools for capitalism, skills for democracy.
4. In the end, however, we must never forget the social, emotional and spiritual needs of all of our children.

Serving the needs/wants of the younger ones in Generation Z. It has come time to rethink the high school curriculum. Let us examine the subjects offered based upon the needs of society as well as the needs of the young person:

1. For participation in capitalism: applied math, computer programming, economics, a foreign language, business management, English composition, technical writing.
2. For participation in democracy: history, civics/government, a foreign language (beginning with Spanish in 2nd grade), offering a 3rd language in 10th grade.
3. For participation in American pluralism: art, music, dance, comparative cultures.
4. For making sense of life: philosophy, comparative religions, world literature, futuristic studies.
5. For connection to self and world: psychology, physical education, sciences (Anatomy, Physiology, Health, Meteorology, Botany, Geology, Geography, Physics, Chemistry, Biology).

PILLAR #7: TOWARDS A COMPLETE EDUCATION

"All human beings are precious and sacred, deserving of respect and love, entitled to the fullest opportunities to develop their intellectual and creative capacities and entitled to be supported in freely choosing and shaping their own life paths" (Lerner 2000).

The next generation's curriculum needs a multipart foundation. I will propose here that the foundational parts are the economic, the political, the social/emotional and the spiritual/intuitive (I did not say religious!).

1. Economic: to contribute to our country's political economy: capitalism
2. Political: to participate in our country's multifaceted community: democracy
3. Social: to navigate well in our pluralistic society
4. Emotional: to find a more satisfying and creative understanding of oneself (the psychological)
5. Spiritual: to make sense of life and one's own life (starting with philosophical inquiry)

For the next generation, school *must* become a place for the *whole* child, not just a place for the development of the mind and the body—basically, today's formal curriculum along with sports or at least PE. It's *not* about blithely stating "no child left behind"; it's about earnestly demanding "no part of the child left out!" We must create a school curriculum *first and foremost for the student*—for the purpose of securing a *deeper* education, not just for advancing many to a *higher* education. It's not just a mind that's a terrible thing to waste; it's a heart and soul that are tragic to ignore.

To move from sublime concerns to more practical ones in advancing this view of education, it is high time to admit that teacher remuneration is completely off in many states. I recently calculated that If I were paid $5/hour simply to *babysit* each student I have every day, then, at an average class size of 26 for a three 1.5 hour periods and one 0.5 hour period (coming out to five hours of direct contact), that (and not at all including prep period nor even the hours of grading after school) would come out to $650/day. Multiply by 170 student days (forgetting the other faculty days per Idaho contract) brings my expected salary to $110,500/year. Which tells me that where I live in the great state of Idaho, I'm massively underpaid. And that's just for babysitting, where my average day these first few years have been 10-hours long (and the usual 15 minutes for lunch).

In a nutshell, it comes to this. *We must not just teach. We must educate!*

And so, many will ask, what's the difference? I will simply explain by using the chef as a metaphor. So that they come to understand that eating a delicious meal (comparable to the actual teaching and learning that everyone remembers from their youth and adolescence) is NOT all that I do. I also prepare the meal (curriculum development, especially in the first 3 years of taking on a new subject to teach), and I also clear the dishes and clean up the kitchen (grading or assessment, especially when new mandates come along).

This is the fundamental problem that prevents the profession from going forward. Who in their right mind is going to take on more interactions per hour, (teachers rank second only to airline traffic controllers in being given decisions that have to be made on the spot), along with the intensity that almost no one understands demanded upon our minds and hearts in a matter of seconds, without having a serious conversation with themselves about cost-benefit? We know the statistics for how many leave the profession after five years. We know that newly minted undergraduates are crazy to consider grades 6–12 teaching here in Idaho at $40,000 per year when they could easily sell themselves to become coders and earn far more!

The time has come to stop the invidious comparisons. For instance, I heard just two years ago at a parent-teacher conference that *I have summers* off (yes, but I simply put in 2000–2200 hours/year in 40 weeks, rather than most Americans who need 50); that *anyone can teach* since the person critiquing said that he taught Sunday school for 5 years (Yes, really?!); and that you have to realize, Dr. Kokol, that the reason you are paid so modestly is that *this is really women's work.* (So, you're still living in the world of *Father Knows Best* and *Leave it to Beaver*?). And with no strikes allowed in this state, what should I expect?

So, it is time for an historic shift in planning for teacher remuneration, the execution of which should wind up making this work, as it was in Horace Mann and Catharine Beecher's generation some 180 years ago, a substantial investment in our infrastructure. No, not our roads. Not even in our high-speed rail lines coming. But in our rising generation. For this might actually repair our broken democracy.

Who would pay for this? Why, that would simply be a reconceptualizing and then reallocating our funds, all easily accomplished with a revamping of our military budget to be more in line with what most Americans want, not what the military-industrial complex lusts after.

The time for these changes—and all the changes I advocate for in this book in the service of children and teachers and in the spirit of John Dewey—is now! Allow me to summarize them here at the end of this extended study in teacher reflectivity (my own!) so that it may serve you, if you choose, as a principled collection of ethical, existential, and pedagogical guidelines from a teacher of four decades at levels spanning high school to the professoriate, from Teton Valley High School to Brigham Young University, to help you chart your course as a teacher at the same time as you are helping your students chart their courses as individuals in this complex world and sacred cosmos.

Table 5.1 The Grand Model

Ideals	Virtues	Powers	Shadows	Failings	Poisons
Truth	Peace	Knowledge	Ignorance	Hostility	Blasphemy
Beauty	Kindness	Imagination	Isolation	Cruelty	Horror
Integrity	Harmony	Reason	Futility	Violence	Hypocrisy
Liberty	Organization	Obedience	Disregard	Rebellion	Agony
Love	Pleasure	Openness	Frustration	Pain	Torment
Joy	Happiness	Confidence	Uncertainty	Sadness	Grief
Humility	Sincerity	Vision	Delusion	Deception	Arrogance
Honor	Respect	Dignity	Defensiveness	Humiliation	Contempt
Faith	Clarity	Purpose	Emptiness	Confusion	Fear
Hope	Compassion	Passion	Vanity	Greed	Despair
Charity	Gratitude	Purpose	Withdrawal	Resentment	Enmity
Wisdom	Enlightened	Curiosity	Confusion	Darkness	Folly

WORKING WITH THE JOURNEY'S TAXONOMY FOR REFLECTIVE PRACTICE AND CURRICULUM DEVELOPMENT

Application 1: Student reflection

Directions:

A. Choose one or two words where you have journeyed recently:

_____   _____

B. Choose one or two words where you would like to be shortly:

_____   _____

C. Study these terms—are they right? How do they make you feel?

_____

D. The take-away here: What can you now see about your journey?

_____

Application 2: Student reflection

A. Self-description
B. Student feedback
C. Can you identify what is holding you back from reaching the top tiers

Application 3: Curriculum development

A. What is the strongest identifiable term within your developed curriculum?
B. What is the weakest identifiable term?
C. What is the main purpose of securing terms for the affective domain in one's lesson?
D. Are there any lessons or sections that need revision to align with terms?

Application 4: New Video ratings system

A. What are the ranges identified by headings of the six columns that your YouTube clips invite students to feel?
B. Are ratings as they currently stand where they need to be?
C. Is there anything too intense for your audience, due to issues relating to maturity policies typically laid out for students under 18?
D. What type of letter to parents would you write to inform them of this taxonomy?

May your journey as a teacher continue to bless you as you continue to bless your students!

References

Adler, M. 1982. *The Paideia Proposal: An Educational Manifesto.* New York: MacMillan.

Apple, M. 2004. *Teachers and Texts.* London: Routledge.

Barzun, J. 2000. *From Dawn to Decadence: 500 Years of Western Cultural Life.* New York: HarperCollins.

Bell, D. 1976. *The Cultural Contradictions of Capitalism.* New York: Basic Books

Bellah, R. 1996. *Habits of the Heart.* Berkeley: University of California Press.

Berliner, D., and B. Biddle. 2003. *The Manufactured Crisis: Myths, Fraud, and the Attack upon America's Public Schools.* Reading, Massachusetts: Addison Wesley.

Bernstein, B. 2000. *Pedagogy, Symbolic Control, and Identity: Theory, Research, Critique.* Lanham, Maryland: Rowman and Littlefield.

Block, A. 1997. *I'm Only Bleeding: Education as the Practice of Social Violence against Children.* New York: Peter Lang.

Bloom, A. 1987. *The Closing of the American Mind.* New York: Simon and Schuster.

Bowles, S., and H. Gintis. 1976. *Schooling in Capitalist America.* New York: Basic Books.

Britzman, D. 2001. *Freud and Education.* London: Routledge.

Bruner, J. 1996. *The Culture of Education.* Cambridge, Mass.: Harvard University Press.

Buber, M. 1965. *I and Thou.* New York: Vintage.

Bullough, R., Jr. 1989. *First-Year Teacher: A Case Study.* New York: Teachers College Press.

Carson, R. 1962. *Silent Spring.* Boston: Houghton Mifflin.

Chardin, T. de. 1975. *The Phenomenon of Man.* New York: Perennial Library.

Cohler, B. 1989. "Psychoanalysis and Education: Motive, Meaning, and Self." In K. Field, B. Cohler, and G. Wool, eds. *Learning and Education: Psychoanalytic Perspectives,* 11–84. Madison, Wisconsin: International Universities Press Inc.

Covey, S. 1989. *Seven Habits of Highly Successful People.* New York: Simon and Schuster.

Cremin, L. 1988. *American Education: The Metropolitan Experience.* New York: Harper and Row.

Cuban, L. 1993. *How Teachers Taught: Constancy and Change in American Classrooms, 1890–1990.* New York: Teachers College Press.

Dewey, J. 1934. *A Common Faith.* New Haven: Yale University Press.

Eisner, E., & B. Vallance. 1985. *The Educational Imagination: On the Design and Evaluation of School Programs.* New York: Macmillan, 1985.

Ekstein, R. 1969. "Psychoanalytic Notes on the Function of the Curriculum." In R. Ekstein and R. Motto, eds. *From Learning for Love to Love of learning: Essays on Psychoanalysis and Education,* 47–57. New York: Brunner/Mazel Publishers.

Eliot, T. 1971. *T.S. Eliot: The Complete Poems and Plays: 1909–1950.* New York: Harcourt, Brace and World, Inc.

Fay, B. 2000. *Contemporary Philosophy of Social Science: A Multicultural Approach.* Oxford: Blackwell Publishers Ltd.

Forbes, S. 2003. *Holistic Education: An Analysis of its Nature and Ideas.* Brandon, Vermont: Foundation for Educational Renewal Press.

Fowler, J. 1981. *Stages of Faith: The Psychology of Human Development and the Quest for Meaning.* San Francisco: Harper and Row.

Gardner, H. 1983. *Frames of Mind.* New York: Basic Books.

Giddens, A. 2002. *Runaway World.* Stanford: Stanford University Press.

Giddens, A. 1990. *The Consequences of Modernity.* Stanford: Stanford University Press.

Goldstein, D. 2014. *The Teacher Wars: A History of America's Most Embattled Profession.* New York: Doubleday.

Heisig. J. 1979. *Imago Dei: A Study of C.G. Jung's Psychology of Religion.* Lewisburg, Pennsylvania: Bucknell University Press.

Herberg, W. 1954. *Protestant, Catholic, Jew: An Essay in American Religious Sociology.* New York: Doubleday.

Homans, P. 1995. *Jung in Context: Modernity and the Making of a Psychology.* Chicago: University of Chicago Press.

Jung, C.G. 1954. *The Symbolic Life.* R. F. C. Hull, Trans. Princeton, New Jersey: Princeton University Press.

Kant, I. 1781/1997. *The Critique of Pure Reason.* Chicago: Hackett Publishing.

Karabel, J. and C. Halsey, eds. A. 1976. *Power and Ideology in Education.* New York: Oxford Press.

Kierkegaard, S. 1969. *A Kierkegaard Anthology.* R. Bretall, ed. Princeton, New Jersey: Princeton University Press.

Kuhn, T. 1970. *The Structure of Scientific Revolutions.* Chicago: University of Chicago Press.

Lasch, C. 1991. *The Culture of Narcissism: American Life in an Age of Diminishing Expectations.* New York: W.W. Norton.

Lerner, M. 2000. *Spirit Matters.* Chicago: Hampton Roads Publishing Company.

Lewis, C.S. 1960. *The Abolition of Man.* New York: Simon and Schuster.

Lickona, T. 1991. *Educating for Character.* New York: Bantam.

Lipman, M. 1988. *Philosophy Goes to School.* Philadelphia: Temple University Press.

Maslow, A. 1968. *Toward a Psychology of Being,* 2nd ed. Princeton, New Jersey: D. Van Nostrand.

Mayes, C. 2020. *Archetype, Culture, and the Individual in Education: The Three Pedagogical Narratives.* Routledge: London.

Mayes, C. 2019. *Developing the Whole Student: New Horizons in Holistic Education.* Lanham, Maryland: Rowman and Littlefield.

Mayes, C. 2012. *Inside Education: Depth Psychology in Teaching and Learning.* Madison, Wisconsin: Atwood Publishing.

Mayes, C. 2004. *Teaching Mysteries: Foundations of a Spiritual Pedagogy.* Lanham, Maryland: University Press of America.

Mayes, C., M. Grandstaff, and A. Fidyk. 2019. *Reclaiming the Fire: Depth Psychology in Teacher Renewal.* Lanham, Maryland: Rowman and Littlefield Press.

McLaren, P. 1998. *Life in Schools: An Introduction to Critical Pedagogy in the Foundations of Education.* (3rd ed.). New York: Longman.

Moe, T., & Chubb, J. 2009. *Liberating Learning: Technology, Politics and the Future of American Education.* San Francisco: Jossey Bass.

Morrow, R., & Torres, C. 1995. *Social Theory and Education: A Critique of Theories of Social and Cultural Reproduction.* Albany, N.Y.: State University of New York Press.

Muggeridge, M. 1971. *Something Beautiful for God: Mother Teresa of Calcutta.* London: Collins.

Osguthorpe, R. 1995. *The Education the Heart.* Provo, Utah: Brigham Young University Press.

Otto, R. 1958. *The Idea of the Holy.* New York: Oxford University Press.

Palmer, P. 1998. *The Courage to Teach: Exploring the Inner Landscape of a Teacher's LIfe.* San Francisco: Jossey-Bass Publishers.

Phenix, P. 1964. *Realms of Meaning: A Philosophy of the Curriculum for General Education.* New York: McGraw-Hill.

Plato. 1960. *The Republic.* New York: Modern Library.

Ravitch, D. and M. Vinovskis, eds. 1995. *Learning from the Past: What History Teaches Us about School Reform.* Baltimore, Maryland: The Johns Hopkins University Press.

Reich, R. 1991. *The Work of Nations: Preparing Ourselves for 21st-Century Capitalism.* New York: A.A. Knopf.

Renzulli, J. 1985.*What Makes Giftedness? A Reexamination of the Definition of the Gifted and Talented.* Ventura, Calif.: Ventura County Superintendent of Schools Office.

Ricoeur, P. 1991. *Freud and Philosophy: An Essay in Interpretation.* New Haven: Yale University Press.

Rilke, R.M. 1934. *Letters to a Young Poet.* New York: Norton.

Rogoff, B. 1990. *Apprenticeship in Thinking: Cognitive Development in Social Context.* New York: Oxford University Press.

Rousseau, J-J. 1763/1950. *The Social Contract, and Discourses.* New York: New American Library.

Rury, J. 1989. "Who Became Teachers? The Social Characteristics of Teachers in American History." In D. Warren, ed. *American Teachers: Histories of a Profession at Work*, 9–48. New York: Macmillan.

Ryan, K. and Bohlin, K. 1998. *Building Character in Schools.* New York: Doubleday.

Saint-Exupery, A. 2001. *The Little Prince.* San Diego: Harcourt.

Salzberger-Wittenberg, I. 1989. *The Emotional Experience of Learning and Teaching.* London: Routledge and Kegan Paul.

Sarason, S. 1999. *Teaching as a Performing Art.* New York: Teachers College Press.

Spring, J. 2006. *American Education* (12th ed). New York: McGraw Hill.

Tillich, P. 1956. *The Essential Tillich.* New York: Macmillan Publishing Co.

Tönnies, F. 1887/1957. *Community and Society.* New York: Harper.

Tyack, D. 1974. *The One Best System: A History of American Urban Education.* Cambridge, Mass.: Harvard University Press.

Veblen, T. 1899/2001. *The Theory of the Leisure Class.* Boston: Houghton Mifflin.

Vinovskis, M. 1985. *The Origin of Public High Schools: A Reexamination of the Beverly High School Controversy.* Madison: University of Wisconsin.

Watras, J. 2005. *The Foundations of Educational Curriculum and Diversity: 1565 to the Present.* Boston: Allyn and Bacon.

Whitehead, A. 1964. *The Aims of Education: And Other Essays.* New York: New American Library.

Winnicott, D.W. 1992. *Psychoanalytic Explorations.* C. Winnicott, R. Shepherd, and M. Davis, eds. Cambridge, Mass.: Harvard University.

About the Author

Martin L. Kokol has been a lifelong educator, primarily teaching 16–24-year-olds in various locales in this country. Being formally recognized as an outstanding teacher by recent students in Idaho, by the Idaho Humanities council, and even the National Endowment of the Humanities at the beginning of his career. From his work during his years as university professor at Brigham Young University, Utah Valley University and Touro College in New York City, he has been able to assemble this work. His current interest lies in gaining a better understanding of spiritual intelligence—something both Steve Covey and Danah Zohar offered over twenty years ago, but was never really followed up on.